UNDERSTANDING SOMALIA
AND SOMALILAND

IOAN M. LEWIS

Understanding Somalia and Somaliland

Culture, History, Society

Columbia University Press
New York

Columbia University Press
Publishers Since 1893
New York
cup.columbia.edu
Copyright © 2008 Ioan M. Lewis

Library of Congress Cataloging-in-Publication Data

Lewis, I. M.
 Understanding Somalia and Somaliland : a guide to cultural history and
social institutions / Ioan M. Lewis.
     p.   cm.
 Includes bibliographical references and index.
 ISBN 978-0-231-70084-9 (cloth : alk. paper)
 ISBN 978-0-231-70085-6 (paperback: alk. paper)
 ISBN 978-0-231-80022-8 (eBook)
 1. Somalia—History. 2. Somaliland (Secessionist government, 1991–)—History. I.
Title.

 DT403.L42 2008
 967.73—dc22

                              2008016919

Columbia University Press books are printed on permanent and durable acid-free paper.
This book is printed on paper with recycled content.
Printed in India

c 10 9 8 7 6 5 4 3 2 1

CONTENTS

Maps   vi

Preface   ix

1 The People and their Traditions   1
2 Colonial Rule and Independence: Nomads and Farmers,
   Socialism and War   27
3 The Collapse in Southern Somalia   71
4 Somaliland and Puntland   93

Appendices
1. *Somali clan families*   109
2. *Bibliography*   110
3. *Glossary of terms*   121
4. *Chronology*   123
5. *Refugees and diaspora*   129

Index   135

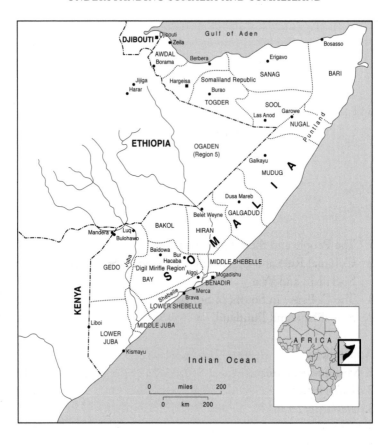

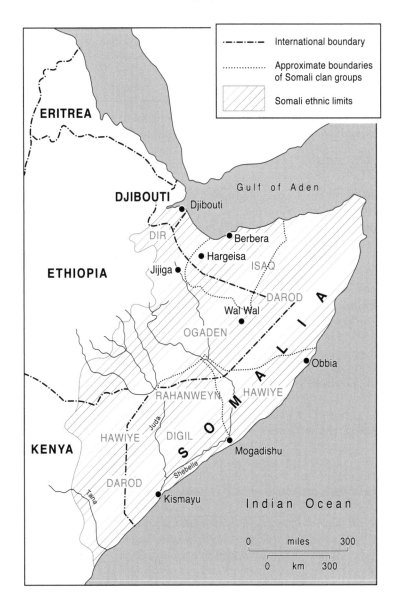

PREFACE

This social anthropological overview of the Somali people, their social institutions and their beliefs, based on first-hand research (as well as documentary evidence) since the 1950s, is intended to provide a brief introduction to key features of Somali life past and present. Originally written in 1978, the text has been exhaustively revised and updated. It now deals at length with the political changes that have befallen Somalia since the overthrow of the dictator General Muhammad Siyad Barre and the state's anarchic collapse in 1990/91.

Given the amount of external intervention since then, it is a depressing commentary on the quality of international engagement that so little of a worthwhile nature has been accomplished. The most positive political achievement has taken place quite independently, without this costly and ineffective international intervention. This is the formation and consolidation of the democratic state of Somaliland which dissolved its union with Somalia in 1991. This self-governing outpost of democracy in Africa, although it has a growing *de facto* personality as an independent state, at the time of writing still seeks international recognition.

This anomaly, as it seems to political leaders in Somaliland, says more about the character of contemporary international affairs than about their own, largely home-made Somali institutions. Following separation from war-torn Somalia in 1991, spontaneous grassroots peace-making enabled Somaliland's clans to achieve substantial political consensus, before their leaders tried to build a government.

This process of local conflict resolution was exactly the opposite of the policy followed by the UN and EC, and other Eurocentric organisations in their many fruitless attempts to re-establish governance in Somalia. Up to the present, their top-down approach, repeated again and again, has failed to provide viable governance in Somalia as was recently acknowledged by the commander of the small Ugandan-manned AU 'peace-keeping' mission to Somalia in 2007. He observed wryly that it was premature to be engaged in peace-keeping when there was neither peace nor visible government in the country.

No wonder those international organisations whose interventions in Somalia have been so unsuccessful should prefer to ignore Somaliland's independent achievements. As Italy was said to be in much of the nineteenth century, Somalia today is little more than a 'geographical expression'. It is consequently difficult to see what purpose is served by continuing to treat Somaliland as formally part of a state that has not been functioning for years. It is misleading and at best simply perpetuates an illusion which distracts attention from the heart of the matter.

The real problem then, and it is acute and exceedingly complicated, is to see how a functioning political structure, government and social services can be restored to the rest of Somalia. Under the regime of transitional President Abdillahi Yusuf, except to a small degree in Puntland, virtually nothing of a serious nature has been achieved. At the moment, there is, however, now a chance that the newly appointed transitional prime minister may be able to make a fresh start. But, if the Transitional Federal Government (TFG) is at last to have some genuine legitimacy, it will obviously be critical to secure a much wider basis of public support than has so far been forthcoming. If Abdillahi Yusuf's Ethiopian allies, whose presence in Somalia is detested, can be got to withdraw from Somalia with as little further disruption and bloodshed as possible, this might help to generate some desperately needed public recognition and approval.

To work, these changes would obviously have to be accompanied by serious negotiation between the TFG leaders and the nationalist rebels in Mogadishu. If this proved at all fruitful, it might be possible to envisage establishing a series of standing local peace conferences in those districts and provinces which were willing to contract into such a widening series of negotiations. These would require to be enduring bodies capable of weathering the local problems and setbacks which would certainly arise.

If such a route were followed, it would of course be crucial to open the existing TFG assembly to new recruits, and to find an acceptable way of demonstrating their representative legitimacy. This would not be achieved by the usual UN and EU declarations of support which carry so little weight with the Somali public. It would also entail a slow process, requiring patience and trust, both alas in short supply. As part of this new 'bottom-up' approach it would ideally make sense to consult the Somaliland authorities about their experience in constructing legislative organisation that has proven suited to Somali conditions. Such contacts might lead to serious discussion about future relations between Mogadishu and Hargeisa. This should include the contested eastern frontier with Puntland and how the local Harti Darod Somali relate to Somaliland and Puntland.

All this, were it adopted, would be liable to attract the interest of UN and EC consultants—although they would probably be deterred by security considerations. That disincentive might be no bad thing since so far such intervention has only been unquestionably helpful in the humanitarian field. There is, however, also another area where, if the wider international community could concentrate its efforts in a really helpful way, its attention would be genuinely beneficial to the Somali people and to other groups in the Horn. This is the obvious issue of arms control. For some years now a UN monitoring committee has recorded the local imports of arms in an exemplary fashion. However, no positive use has been made of this data which could at least guide valuable discussions between the Horn of Africa regional authority and members of the UN assembly. So many of the countries political-ly engaged in the Horn of Africa have commercial interests here that this may seem an impossible issue to raise. But arms supply is such an obvious impediment to effective government that this problem has to be tackled

In this short book, I have sought to emphasise the pervasive influence in the contemporary Somali world of the traditional no-madic background and its extremely de-centralised character. This brief introduction to a very complex people and their country is, naturally, no substitute for firsthand experience. I hope, however, that it may help to make such experience informed and fruitful.

I am grateful to the former specialist Somali publisher Anita Adam for suggesting this new, expanded edition and for contrib-uting the appendix on refugees, and to Professor Said Samatar of Rutgers University whose analytical understanding of Somali so-ciety and culture is unrivalled. I would also like to thank a number of other friends whose comments on the manuscript have im-proved this text, especially Dr Abdi Salan Ise Salwe, Dr Michael Brophy, Sally Healey, Edward Mason, Dr Umar Duhood, and Susan Willock.

In rendering Somali terms generally in the text my orthography follows standard Somali usage, without, however, indicating long vowels. Thus the sounds of Somali words spelt as shown can be quite accurately grasped.

LSE, March 2008   I.M. Lewis

1

THE PEOPLE AND THEIR TRADITIONS

The Somali ethnic region

With a total population estimated at about 8 million, the Somali people traditionally occupy a large expanse of territory in the
Horn of Africa, stretching from the Awash valley in the north to
beyond the Tana river in northern Kenya in the south. Of these,
following the collapse of Somalia in 1990, as many as two million
people were at the time of writing believed to be resident outside
their homeland as refugees distributed widely in Africa, the Middle East, Europe, and North America.

In terms of linguistic and cultural affiliation, Somalis belong
ethnically to the Cushitic-speaking family. This grouping includes
the neighbouring Afar (or Danakil, or Ooda'ali as Somalis call
them) of Djibouti, Eritrea and the Awash Valley, and the numerous Oromo and Borana of Ethiopia and Northern Kenya (known
formerly by the derogatory term 'Galla').

Migration and the Islamic tradition

With a long tradition of trading connections to the Arabian
Peninsula, the Somalis were converted to Islam at an early date

and remain staunch Muslims (Sunnis, of the Sha'afi School of Law). This is reflected in the traditional practice of tracing descent from illustrious Arab ancestors connected with the family of the Prophet Muhammad. Its modern expression can be seen in Somalia's membership, since 1974, of the Arab League.

According to some linguistic criteria, an earlier movement of 'Proto-Somali' speakers brought the language from Ethiopia to the Horn, before the general drift of the Somali population from north to south (see Lewis 2002, p. 312, note 2). One of the major routes in this latter movement has been from the northeast coast of the Sanag Region, where some of the legendary founders of the main clan groups are believed to be buried. Another principal route, frequently mentioned in the oral tradition, is by way of the ancient Islamic citadel of Harar, where tombs venerated as those of the ancestors of other Somali groups lie.

Over a thousand years ago, Arab and Persian trading settlements (where goods came from as far afield as China) had been established at such coastal centres as Zeila in the north (on the route to Harar) and in the south at Mogadishu (where the great mosque dates from the thirteenth century). Further south along the coast Merca and Brava are of similar antiquity. These Muslim centres of commerce, reinforcing the Islamic identity of the Somali people, also appear to have given an additional impetus to population movements towards the west and south.

As far as documentary evidence is concerned, Somalis first came into secure focus in the written records of the Middle Ages. Eyewitnesses documented their role in the protracted 'holy wars' (*jihad*s), which raged in the late Middle Ages between Christian Ethiopia and the surrounding Islamic sultanates. At their peak in the sixteenth century, from his base in Harar, the great Islamic leader Ahmad Gurey ('Ahmad the left-handed', known to the Ethiopians as 'Ahmad Grañ') briefly conquered much of the central Abyssinian highlands. The recovery of Christian Ethiopia was decisively helped by the intervention of their Christian allies the Portuguese. Somali participation in these wars remains a vivid part of folk consciousness in the region, particularly since the Islamic hero's lieutenant was a Somali of the same name. These two figures, who are clearly distinguished in the Arabic chronicles of the time, are often confused in the oral tradition.

The traditional centres of Islam, seats of early Arab immigration and settlement, are the towns of Harar (with its urban Semitic tongue) in the north-west highlands, its ancient port Zeila, and in the south Mogadishu (known to Somalis as 'Hamar': one of the two original divisions of the city bears the same name), Merca, and Brava (whose ancient city population speaks a Swahili-related dialect called 'Chimbalazi'). Mogadishu's earliest mosques are among the oldest on the East African coast.

The Somali nation and its traditional divisions

The majority of Somalis belong traditionally to a pastoral nomadic culture, herding camels (the traditional prestige wealth), sheep and goats and, in favourable regions, cattle. Some 60 to 70 per cent of the population are nomadic or have nomadic affiliation, even though many today live in urban centres for part of the time at least. Most of the remainder, who farm, also keep livestock. A much smaller proportion of the population, primarily living in the urban coastal communities, has its traditional economic base in commerce (*see below*) and fisheries.

The distinction between nomad and cultivator coincides roughly with the most marked internal cultural division in the Somali nation. The fertile area between the Shebelle and Juba rivers is occupied mainly by farmers and agro-pastoralists who, while they often understand the standard spoken Somali current elsewhere, speak their own distinctive tongue, known as Af-Maymay. (Although often referred to as a 'dialect', this is properly a not-mutually-intelligible language, related to Somali.) These people form two confederations of clans called Digil and Rahanweyn, or Digil Mirifle, known collectively, in some parts of Somalia, as Sab. As the name Rahanweyn ('large crowd') suggests, the Sab are of mixed origin, and include elements drawn from almost all the other Somali groups, as well as some Oromos and East African Bantu. (Ex-slave Bantu individuals, living amongst Rahanweyn clans, often work as manual labourers engaged in house construction and other building work.)

The Digil Mirifle social structure is based on the adoption or assimilation of foreign clansmen to a local clan core whose name and identity the immigrants assume, thus acquiring local land rights. Those who genuinely descend from the founding ancestors in any group are today often a tiny minority, but nevertheless retain their status through the system of expansion of the group with successive layers of adopted clients. The Digil Mirifle are thus the most open and politically hospitable of all Somali groups. Indeed their heterogeneous 'melting pot' organisation makes them theoretically an ideal model for Somali nationalism. For various reasons, however, including the nomads' vigorous genealogical pride and traditional scorn for cultivators, this potential has not been used as a valid basis for modern Somali nationalism whose main proponents have been drawn from nomadic culture. Had the Digil Mirifle enjoyed a higher national status, and included fewer people of non-Somali origin (e.g. fewer ex-slaves and people of other servile categories), the situation might have been different.

The other main branches of the nation are respectively the Dir, Isaq, Hawiye and Darod. Strictly speaking, the Isaq are derived historically from the Dir, who together with the Hawiye are linked as 'Irir' at a higher level of genealogical grouping. In terms of their multi-functional lineage organisation, based on descent traced exclusively in the male line, these pastoralist groups provide the stereotype of traditional Somali socio-political organisation. Despite local variations, they are the quintessential Somalis.

The Somali nation as a whole thus consists of six main divisions, which are to some extent geographically distinct. The main

Dir clans, principally the Esa and Gadabursi, are in the Harar-Borama-Zeila area; but the Biamal (or Bimal) are a historically important Dir group based round Merca in southern Somalia. The neighbours of the Dir in the northwest are the Isaq (whose centre is now the Somaliland Republic) who, in turn, live next to the Darod, the largest and most widely distributed of all the Somali groups. The members of this huge clan-family inhabit northeastern Somalia (now known as 'Puntland'), northeastern Kenya, and the Ogaden region of eastern Ethiopia ('Western Somalia') which is named after one of their most famous clans. In post-revolutionary Ethiopia this is known administratively as 'Region Five'. The Somali hero and famous oral poet Sayyid Muhammad Abdille Hassan, the so-called 'Mad Mullah' who from 1900 to 1920 waged a holy war against the Christian colonisers of his country (and others who did not share his fundamentalist views), belonged to this clan (*see below*).

The Hawiye in turn occupy the Hiran and Mudug regions of Somalia and part of the Benadir (or southern coastal littoral and its hinterland), where Mogadishu, the capital city, is located. (Some Hawiye have assumed control of Benadir areas in the course of the ongoing 'civil war' in southern Somalia.) However, as an ancient trading port Mogadishu or 'Hamar' has long been cosmopolitan. From the early twentieth century it included representatives of most Somali groups in addition to its own distinctive ancient Arab-Somali city populations known as Rer Hamar (literally 'people of Mogadishu'). These long-urbanised communities practised a range of trades including gold and silver working, shoemaking and leather working, weaving and fishing. There were also Ashraf (descendants of the Prophet) and other specialist religious groups. Beyond Mogadishu, Hawiye clans stretch across the Shebelle river into the region occupied by the Digil and Rahanweyn, where some have become farmers. Along with various nomadic Darod clans, they are also found across the Juba river and in northeastern Kenya.

These main cultural divisions—nomadic pastoralist and culti-vator—include significant numbers of people generally referred to by Somalis by a variety of derogatory names associated with servile status, and known by foreigners as 'minorities'. These do not strictly belong genealogically to the two main populations, but live in association with them, traditionally under their protec-tion and sometimes in various stages of assimilation. Physically the most distinctive are those known generally as Jareer (or 'hard haired')—Somalised Bantu, who derive from pre-Somali popula-tions, and more recent immigrant Eastern Swahili groups origi-nally brought to Somalia as slaves.

From these sources, various hybrid Somali-style groups have developed in the inter-riverine area and along the Shebelle and Juba river basins. Some are bilingual in southern Somali (Af-Maymay) and Swahili. Typical examples are the Shidle and She-belle and other smaller agricultural communities settled along the Shebelle river, and the Gobaweyn and WaGosha at opposite ends of the Juba river. The last named—who were given this name from the Swahilised version of the Somali Rer Gol, 'people of the for-est', referring to the wooded banks (gol) of the Juba river as they were in the nineteenth century—are famous in local history for their chief, Nasib Bunda, who after valiantly championing their independence was taken prisoner by the Italian colonisers.

The Boni are a scattered hunting and fishing people found along, and between, the southern ends of both rivers. Another famous hunting group, also renowned for their pottery, are the Eyle of Bur Heibe, near Baidoa between the rivers. Although pas-toralist Somalis despise hunting, they are impressed by the deadly potency of the Eyle's poison-tipped arrows. During the savage wars waged by Hawiye and Darod warlords and their clan militias in southern Somalia after the collapse of the state in 1990, these traditionally despised groups, largely dependent on farming for their livelihood and having no armed militias to defend them, were mercilessly slaughtered, and many sought asylum overseas.

Indeed, several large groups of Jareer eventually found refuge in the United States, where they were welcomed as victims of racist oppression.

Besides the Jareer, with whom Somali pastoralists do not intermarry, other occupational specialists of low status are the hunters, leather-workers (e.g. shoemakers) and metal craftsmen known respectively as Yibir, Midgans, and Tumals. These craft specialists have sometimes been reported as speaking languages separate and distinct from standard Somali. My field research does not confirm this claim, although they do sometimes utilise their own slang when they wish to communicate secretly, and they have their own songs and poetry. They are known collectively as Sab (but are not related to the Digil Mirifle), and are generally regarded snobbishly by pastoralist Somali as 'unclean'. (However, as a pioneering serological analysis by Goldsmith and Lewis in 1958 demonstrated, there appears to be no significant difference between blood samples of sab and standard Somali people.)

Various pastoralist myths purport to explain these peoples' low status as a fall from grace caused by eating unclean (haram) meat during a famine. As individuals or families practising their specialist crafts, these groups traditionally lived as 'bondsmen' attached to pastoralist patrons who were responsible for their protection. The extent to which they were exploited by their patrons appears to have varied widely.

The numbers of low-status groups, past and present, are hard to estimate, but in the 1960s there were thought to be under 15,000 in Somalia and Somaliland, dispersed among the general population. The larger groups, such as the Midgans, developed neo-lineage organisation, modelled on the Somali system but operating on a much smaller scale. Since independence in 1960 their status has gradually improved, and a few notable individuals attached to major pastoralist clans became prominent politicians on the national stage as well as famous singers or poets, an earlier route to fame and fortune. General Muhammad Siyad Barre's Senior

Vice President and Minister of Defence, General Muhamad Ali Samatar, trained in Russia, was a high profile Tumal. Judging from politically incorrect comments made, *sotto voce*, by various Somali commentators, General Samatar's origins made it unlikely that he could head a successful coup against Siyad: and he appears never to have tried. Under the modern title 'Gabboye', and claiming that like other Somalis they have their own clans, *sab* have also achieved political representation in contemporary politics (*see below*). By the year 2000 their status, although still ambiguous, had become in practice less ascribed and more dependent on individual and family achievement. But they still lacked the axiomatic support enjoyed by members of powerful large pastoralist clans, with their well-armed militias.

Their gradual rise in status was linked with the increasing extension of urban life from its historic roots in the Benadir region of southern Somalia, south of Mogadishu and around the ports of Mogadishu, Merca and Brava, and Kismayu and the coastal villages in between, where sundry low status (i.e. non-pastoralist) specialist craft communities had developed from the original Arab settlers. This coastal region, known from this Arab presence as Benadir (from the Arabic plural 'ports'), gave its name in local usage in the form Benadiri, as well as the Somali collective format *'Rer Benadir'*, to designate a person living here. Hence developed the usage 'Af-Benadir', literally 'Benadir language', applied to the local patois version of southern Somali (see Moreno 1955, preface). The terminology used by refugees in the UK (and adopted in the British Home Office jargon) followed the all-embracing Somali clan logic which assumes that all collections of people are 'clans'. So it treated those who come from the Benadir region as yet another Somali clan and referred to them as 'Benadir' as though this was equivalent to other Somali clans. But this term, designating essentially a region, did not formally describe a clan, or even a community.

What the ancient, Somalised Arab population of these urban centres has in common is minority social status, on the fringe of mainstream warrior pastoralist Somali society. All the component urban groups (the Rer Benadir, in the largest conception) are relatively small and have no traditional military organisation for self-defence. They have, thus, always been at the mercy of armed predatory groups, and subjected to colonisation, over the centuries, by successive waves of pastoralist invaders attracted by the desire to control the prosperous Benadir. In modern times, its trading ventures have made this region the most valuable in Somalia, and hence especially attractive to the marauding clans from the north who fell upon Mogadishu as the state collapsed.

Traditionally, as in the case of the largest Benadir town Mogadishu (Hamar), the component Rer Hamar 'clans' (in anthropological terms, free-standing 'descent groups' without any lineage-based internal structure) are aligned in loosely organised alliances, similar to East African urban moieties. Their orally preserved genealogies, unlike those of the Somali pastoralists, seldom extend over more than four or five generations, and marriage is typically with a fairly close cousin (on the father's or mother's side). So this ancient urban population of Mogadishu, with tomb inscriptions going back to the eighth century, traces its origins to Arabia—appropriately, more immediately, and probably more authentically, than the pastoralist clans. It is historically divided into two territorial divisions: Hamarweyn (lit. 'old, or greater' Mogadishu) and Shangani. Hamarweyn is traditionally composed of four groups (loosely organised by descent): the Morshe, the Iskashatto, the Dabbarweyn and the Bandabbow. Each of these in turn has its own attached accessory groups (e.g. the Hatimi, Aydarus, Durukbo, Shanshiye and Kalmashubbe, and Gudmane).

These groups are all mixed in composition, and largely synthetic assemblages of adopted people. Thus, while the majority are dark-skinned (*gibil madow*) like the dominant Somali, a few are light-skinned (*gibil 'ad*) and some are a mixture. They pursue a variety of crafts: metal and leather working, weaving the local *alindi* ('India') cloth, silver and gold working, fishing and general trading. A particular group does not exclusively practice a distinctive craft. In disputes with other groups, the 'Four Hamarweyn' paid and received compensation for injuries and death (*mag, diig*) collectively, as did the 'Five Shangani'. The latter comprised the Yaqub, Ashraf, Amudi, Saddeh Gedi and Rer Manjo. The last, called the 'sea people', were primarily engaged in fishing and selling fish. All the others practiced a similar mixture of crafts, cash crops, and commerce. None of these groups had substantial holdings of livestock, and their culture (admitting a few domestic sheep and goats and poultry) was decidedly urban and, in their rituals, focused primarily on the sea and the ancient (pre-Islamic) new year festival *nayrus*. This is also known as *is-tunka*, and is celebrated in a large-scale communal performance at Afgoi on the Shebelle river outside Mogadishu. Although they traded with it, their urban world was quite separate from the world of the dominant pastoralists who alone possessed weapons and ultimately exercised political control. Their most successful traders were undoubtedly among the richest individuals in the Somali population, and their constant involvement in money transactions, however small, fostered among the pastoralists the idea that these poorly protected urban dwellers had limitless wealth.

As they are sedentary people, the material culture of the Rer Hamar resembles that of coastal Arabia, and is perhaps most clearly differentiated from that of the pastoralists by their handsome three- or four-storied coral and stone houses. It was only in 1920, under the Italians, that the ancient city wall bounding Hamarweyn and Shangani was destroyed, opening the town to the marauding pastoralists who, during and after the overthrow of President Siyad Barre in 1991, eventually destroyed it. These magnificent buildings (some of which partially survived the ensuing 'civil war') are divided into apartments, enabling an extended family of several generations to occupy several floors of the same building.

Although their urban style of life was (until substantially destroyed in the 'civil war') best represented by the Rer Hamar of Mogadishu, many features were shared with the similar, Arab-derived core urban populations of the other Benadir ports: Merca, Brava, and Kismayu. Tradition records that the original founders of Brava, the 'Hatimi', came from Yemen by sea. Eventually, a Somali group called Tunni wrested power from them and established themselves largely as farmers on the rich arable land outside the city. This they held in common and worked with the aid of Bantu 'slaves' imported, as they record, from East Africa and those settled on the Shebelle river. The Tunni are divided into two groups, the Tunni Shan Gamas (i.e. 'five shields') and the subordinate Tunni Torre, with a higher proportion of attached ex-slaves. The livestock of the Tunni is largely restricted to cattle and sheep and goats.

With a similarly mixed economy, much the same pattern of life prevailed in the riverine town of Afgoi, the Benadir centre for the famous new year festival known locally as *dabshid* and *istun* (see Luling, 2002). This town and its surrounding fields are particularly interesting in being part of a traditional alliance between the politically dominant Geledi (Digil), who created the leading indigenous city-state in southern Somalia, and the associated Hawiye Wa'adan clan. This cross-clan alliance was a rare phenomenon in Somalia.

Family organisation

The Somalis are traditionally polygynous, marrying, according to the Islamic code, a maximum of four wives at any one time. The number of wives a man has varies generally with age, seniority being associated with more wives. The actual incidence of polygyny varies widely: among both the pastoral nomads and the southern Digil and Rahanweyn the majority of men will probably have had at least two wives at some point in their lives, and the rich and successful will often have had four. Since marriage is extremely unstable, with a high frequency of divorce, the number of marriages contracted in the course of the average man's life is actually often far higher than these statements would indicate. A significantly higher proportion of the male population will have contracted half a dozen marriages or more before they die; others will have contracted many more than this. The primary aim of marriage is to produce children, especially male heirs who will add strength and honour to a father's lineage and enhance his reputation and status. There are elders with 100 or more living descendants. In a harsh environment with a high infant mortality rate and extreme climatic uncertainties, the Somalis recognise that, as with their livestock husbandry, they overproduce their human population to offset natural hazards. Since at all levels in the population fighting strength and political muscle are a matter of force of numbers, optimum size is the constant goal. These attitudes, widely prevalent in the population, are not conducive to modern birth control schemes.

In the polygynous pastoralist family, each wife and her children form a separate socio-economic unit with their own dwelling and small stock (sheep and goats). In the case of farmers, if a man has ample land it is divided into separate plots: if land is scarce the wives work in the same plot, but the harvest is divided among them. Each uterine family (*has* or *ras*) within the polygynous family (*hasas* or *rasas*) is called *bah*, its children being full siblings but only paternal half-siblings to the children of other families. The first wife is the senior (*bahweyn* or *minweyn*), her children being the firstborn (*'urad'*); she heads the family of wives and, traditionally, keeps the keys of the family money-box. Since, although Islam enjoins them to treat their wives equally, men tend to favour the youngest and most physically attractive marriage partner, there is much jealousy and friction among co-wives and their children.

Indeed the word co-wife (*dangalo*) also means jealousy (literally: those whose interests cross).

The relative seniority of wives and their children is reflected in the precedence of the first wife's family in distribution of the joint family income and in inheritance rights. In the traditional Islamic inheritance rules, female heirs have fewer rights than male heirs. In practice among the Somali, although women might inherit housing, land and small stock, they rarely acquired possession of camels, which are treated as a male preserve. A new 'family law' (*herka qoyska*), introduced by Siyad's 'Scientific Socialist' regime in 1975, gave female heirs the same rights as male heirs, though the extent to which this is followed among pastoral nomads is debatable. Certainly male superiority is still taken for granted, men regularly walking before their wives who follow at a respectful distance behind.

The sexual division of labour, with women assigned the husbandry of sheep and goats while men deal with grazing camels, emphasises these chauvinistic attitudes which are further reinforced in the *machismo* honour code, stressing the vulnerability and chastity of women. But women, particularly among the nomads, are traditionally not veiled (although since the 1980s an increasing number are in towns) and enjoy considerable freedom of movement and independence in the management of sheep and goats. Women also usually are found looking after the burden camels which carry the pastoralists' tents and possessions from place to place. They thus habitually deal with the most bad-tempered and aggressive of Somali livestock. So perhaps it is not surprising that women tend to be forceful characters who often exercise more influence than appears on the surface. As might be expected, these trends have increased, particularly in recent years in towns where, for example, the incidence of arranged marriage declined markedly, while with the growing influence of fundamentalism from the 1980s it became more common for women to wear the veil.

Marriage arrangements

Historically, marriage among the nomads (with some exception in the case of the Mijerteyn clansmen) was usually outside the *diya*-paying group, the basic kinship-based political unit. This reflected the political significance of marriage as an alliance between potentially hostile groups and was sometimes included in peace treaties (as for example in the peace deals between clans which formed the basis of the new Somaliland Republic in 1991/92). This political aspect inspired the main marriage payments (*yarad*) from the groom's group to the wife's family, and the return gift (*dibad*) made at, or after the actual wedding. These transactions involve traditionally large numbers of livestock, especially camels, and other items of prestige wealth (e.g. horses and guns), including money. The return presents brought by the bride from her kin include the marriage house (*aros*) and, typically, a flock of sheep and goats to supply milk to the children of the union and burden camels to transport the family from place to place.

The crucial Islamic element uniting the couple as man and wife is the *mahar*, or witnessed contract, according to which the groom undertakes to pay his wife jewellery of an agreed value in cash or kind. Despite its religious significance, this is often only actually paid on divorce, and so acts as a divorce surety for the wife—although its material value may be slight.

Among the southern agricultural Somalis (Digil and Rahanweyn) marriage is a less costly undertaking. Here the main transaction is the *mahar*, and it is usually the groom's rather than bride's family that supplies the matrimonial house. Marriage partners, at the same time, are not chosen from remote groups. Indeed there is a strong preference for marriage with a paternal or maternal cousin. This may help to integrate these heterogeneous groups which consist of so many different clan elements. Among pastoralists and farmers, though more in the case of the former, if a husband dies his widow may be inherited by the deceased husband's brother or other close relative. This 'widow inheritance' is called *dumal*. Similarly, a widower has some entitlement to a replacement bride (*higsisan*).

These practices underline the corporate rather than purely personal nature of marriage as an alliance, especially among the pastoral nomads. This is also seen in the fact that unmarried women are an important currency in inter-lineage peace agreements; their surrender as brides between the parties cements an agreement, promising a future generation strongly bound to both sides. Such political marriages played a significant part in the peace negotiations leading to the formation of the new Somaliland Republic in the 1990s (see Ahmed Yusuf Farah in Lewis 2008).

Traditionally, Benadiri marriages were, ideally, arranged in a similar fashion by the elder kinsmen of the spouses, and Arab-style cousin marriage was usually practised following infant betrothal. All this emphasised the locally rooted character of Benadir family and social organisation, with the absence of the wide-ranging alliances of the pastoralists.

Elopement seems to have been a common way of avoiding such arranged marriages. More recent social and economic changes have impacted variously at different times on these traditional practices. Following independence in 1960, and the sense of freedom that it brought, the urban trend among young working people was towards choosing their own marriage partners, a trend that was no doubt influenced by freer-thinking contemporaries returning from Western education overseas. The impact was felt particularly in the 1970s and 80s, and encouraged by the 'revolutionary-period' government of Siyad Barre. The trend away from arranged marriages continued, with partnerships often being forged from beyond the conventional range of accepted cross-clan arrangements, but again this was more common among the recently urbanised groups, and had less marked effect on marriage patterns in the interior or among the traditional urban communities. In the decades since the civil war, however, with the need for clans and groups to coalesce protectively around mutual interests, this trend was reversed, and more traditional partnerships and arranged marriages were for the time being the norm. Indeed, in the wake of the seemingly endless 'civil war', marriage with different and potentially or actually hostile descent-groups was no longer popular.

Religion and general cultural characteristics

The Somalis are firmly attached to Islam and divided traditionally into three main denominations: the Qadiriya, the Ahmadiya, and an Ahmadiya derivative, the Salihiya. These are the Sufi or mystical brotherhoods (*turuq*, sing. *tariqa*) found throughout the Muslim world, the Qadiriya being the oldest and least puritanical. The Salihiya is a nineteenth-century reformist movement with a fundamentalist orientation, owing its importance to the fact that the national hero, Sayyid Muhammad Abdille Hassan, waged his crusade against the Christian colonisers under its banner. The Qadiriya has, however, a larger number of followers.

Few Somalis are formal initiates of these religious movements. Their founders have, however, been assimilated into the Somali calendar of saints (including local clan founders like Sheikhs Darod and Isaq) and their sheikhs act as local religious leaders and teachers. Other local saints, such as Sharif Yusuf Al-Qoniin (widely known as Aw Barkhadle, 'blessed one') who is venerated at shrines in southern Somalia and Somaliland, are the subject of important local pilgrimages. Such is his mystical blessing that three successive pilgrimages to his shrine in the north (some twenty miles from Hargeisa) are considered to be equivalent to going on the *haj* once to Mecca. This pioneering Muslim missionary, who probably came to Somaliland in the twelfth century, is also said to have visited the Bay region of southern Somalia where he is known as Qonton Barkhadle ('fifty times blessed'). Sharif Yusuf is said to have encountered non-Muslim Oromo here and challenged them to a trial of mystical power which, through the saint's superior blessing (*baraka*), resulted in the turning to stone and imprisonment of the Oromo leader in Mount Heibe. A very similar tradition commemorates his appearance in Somaliland where Sharif Yusuf is also credited with the introduction of the Arabian black-headed, fat-tailed sheep, bred throughout Somali territory today, and the invention of a Somali notation for the Arabic vowels, facilitating the teaching of Arabic (see Lewis 1998, chap. 7).

Although the Salihiya sang hymns addressed to their leader, Sayyid Muhammad Salih, as though to a saint (*wali*), after his death his grave was not treated or venerated as a shrine (*qabri*). Similarly, while mystical power had sometimes been attributed to him during his life, after his death Sayyid Muhammad Abdille Hassan was not venerated as a saint. This was in line with Salihiya fundamentalist tenets and opposition to the Somali cult of saints, in contrast to the Qadiriya, and a major point of contention between them. Hostility between the two orders was such that each denounced the other as infidel and they descended to open warfare. The Qadiriya were accused of supporting the Christian colonisers, and in 1909 a raiding party of Sayyid Muhammad's followers fiercely attacked the headquarters of the southern Qadiriya leader, Sheikh Uways, at Bioley in southern Somalia, killing the saint and a number of his prominent disciples (see S.S. Samatar, 1992). Since this murder, the sheikh's tomb at Bioley has become one of the most important pilgrimage centres in Somalia.

The 'Dervish War' as it was called, of which this episode was part, dominated life in the fledgling Somaliland Protectorate and surrounding territories. This was indeed the first sustained anti-colonial campaign, lasting from 1900 to 1920 when its leader died of natural causes in a remote camp among his clansmen, the Ogaden. This brought the movement back to the region of its origin where it had first been ignited by the invasion of Ethiopian troops, sent out to extend the Ethiopian empire.

17

The extraordinarily protracted persistence of the Sayyid's campaign, despite concerted opposition from the British, Italians and Ethiopians, and sporadic conflict with hostile Somali clans and groups were a remarkable testimony to the Sayyid's success as a guerrilla leader. Successfully exploiting his skills in desert warfare, he ruthlessly pursued his ultimate aim, the riddance from his country of the 'infidels', as he called the Christian colonisers. At the time Britain was weakened militarily by involvement in the Boer War but nevertheless, with varying degrees of success, mounted four military expeditions against the Dervishes between 1900 and 1920. The last expedition included the first use in Africa—apart from North Africa—of air support, and entailed high costs and high casualties.

The Sayyid's successful defiance of his adversaries for so long was in the Somali context partly due to the brilliance of his political propaganda expressed in the telling medium of Somali oral poetry of which he was, without question, one of the most accomplished exponents of his age (see S.S. Samatar 1982). His famous tirade against the British Camel Corps commander Richard Corfield (who was killed in a particularly ferocious engagement with the Dervishes in 1913) gives such a chilling example of the Sayyid's style that it merits quoting here in translation:

You have died, Corfield, and are no longer in this world;
A merciless journey was your portion,
When hell-destined, you set out for the Other World,
Those who have gone to Heaven will question you if God is willing;
When you see the Companions of the Faith-
full and the jewels of Heaven,
Answer them how God tried you,
Say to them: 'From that day to this, the der-
vishes never ceased their assaults upon us.
The British were broken, the noise of battle engulfed us;
With fervour and faith the Dervishes attacked us.'

Say: 'They attacked us at mid-morning'.
Say: 'Yesterday in the holy war, a bul-
let from one of their old rifles struck me.
And the bullet struck me in the arm.'
Say: 'In fury they fell upon us.'
Report how savagely their swords tore you;
Show these past generations in how many
places the daggers were plunged.
Say: 'Friend, I called, "Have compassion and spare me!"'

(from B.W. Andrzejewski and I.M. Lewis 1964, p. 72)

Although the puritanical Salihiya-inspired *jihad* was the most important fundamentalist movement in twentieth-century Somali Islam, it had an earlier, if less directly anti-colonial counterpart in southern Somalia, based at the Islamic centre of Bardera on the middle reaches of the Juba river, established by a local sheikh in 1819. It is not entirely clear that the sheikh's doctrinal orientation was directly associated with the Ahmadiya Order (of which the Salihiya is a branch), but his reformist zeal is clear. He outlawed the use of tobacco and proscribed folk dancing, especially where it involved women and men mixing. Women were instructed to wear the veil. Interestingly, the local ivory trade was forbidden on the grounds that the elephant was an unclean (*haram*) animal. In the mid-1830s, Bardera's holy war took on an expansive character; the people of the walled city sent their forces to attack the surrounding clans, thus upsetting the Sultan of the Geledi at Afgoi, near Mogadishu, who in this period was the major leader in southern Somalia. Retaliation followed swiftly. In the 1840s the Geledi Sultan, Yusuf Muhamad, assembled a huge force of some 40,000 warriors from his own and allied clans. This marched to Bardera and besieged the town. After only a few days, the town was seized and burnt down: all its inhabitants were killed or fled. So ended the *jihad* until the flame was rekindled, as we have seen, at the end of the century by Sayyid Muhammad Abdille Hasan,

19

whose holy war initially focused primarily on the Ethiopians before confronting all the Christian colonisers.

The latest fundamentalist movement in this tradition began in the late 1980s and early 1990s when contemporary Arab missionaries, Wahhabi and other, with Saudi Arabian, Sudanese or Iranian connections and resources (including modern weapons), began to compete for followers among those Somalis who were reacting to the terrible scourges their country had suffered in this period.

With the collapse of their state in 1990, after Siyad Barre's dictatorship, some welcomed the Arabian fundamentalist Wahhabi al-Ittihad al-Islam which challenged the traditional cult of saints of the established Qadiriya order, just as Sayyid Muhammad Abdille Hassan had done in his conflict with the colonialists at the turn of the twentieth century. These contemporary fundamentalists similarly questioned the claims made for the therapeutic powers of traditional saints. One of the commonest and oldest remedies here was the drinking of healing potions prepared by washing a freshly written Quranic text into a cup. This ingestion of Holy Writ was, of course, considered especially effective when it had been transcribed by a famous holy man. Most other magical remedies depended for their effectiveness on their connection with the Quran and other sources of Islamic power. The popular cult of saints, and the therapeutic powers of charms and amulets charged with verses from the Quran, traditionally played an important part in daily life.

Here we encounter the complementary relationship that Somalis traditionally see between the laity and the religious. This is expressed in the terms 'man of God' (i.e sheikh/priest) and 'warrior' (*wadad iyo waranleh*, lit. 'spear-bearer'). In contrast to the situation among the Arabs, the title 'sheikh', designating a *wadad* of superior learning, does not mean a political leader or 'chief', a position generally alien to the highly egalitarian Somali. Religious teachers and leaders (*wadads)* mediate between man and God, and between men. For an appropriate fee, they are expected to dispense blessings and magical potions, to bless livestock, crops, women—and so contribute to their fecundity—and to conduct all religious services, including weddings, funerals, and sacrifices (e.g. in rain-making).

This distinction between arms-bearing laity and pacific, mystically empowered religious specialists is often violated in practice when religious figures become directly involved in fighting. The tension here can of course be resolved when recourse to arms is in a religious cause, as in the Dervish campaign against the Christian colonisers, led by Sayyid Muhammad Abdille Hassan. Similarly, and much more recently, in 2007 when the Islamic jurists who briefly assumed power in Somalia sought to consolidate their somewhat inchoate polities, they found a convenient cause for *jihad* in the threat posed by 'Christian' Ethiopia. As we shall see in a later section, this 'religious' confrontation lasted only a matter of days until the Ethiopian armoured troops with superior equipment and air support rolled in, and the Islamists scattered. Although victorious for the time being, in the Muslim Somali moral perspective the Ethiopians and the Somali secularists they supported had cast themselves beyond the pale. The legitimacy of the Muslim cause was firmly re-established to remain a lasting justification for future religious 'rebellion'.

While popular Somali Islam includes belief in the powers (generally malevolent) of wayward spirits which are especially attracted to women, witchcraft is not a prominent force as in most African cultures. Spirit possession illnesses (*sar* or *mingis)* in women can be treated either by exorcism or by initiation into women's ritual groups which are commoner in towns than in rural society (see Lewis 2003, pp. 90ff.). The treatment of these afflictions is costly and falls most heavily on the male next of kin—husbands and fathers and, in the case of unmarried women, brothers. Men sceptically regard these afflictions in their womenfolk as devices which the subordinated sex uses against the dominant male.

This sceptical, or at best ambiguous, attitude toward mystical power is characteristic of the Somalis who, while acknowledging that God is the ultimate causal force in the universe, prudently also seek more immediate causes and remedies. There is thus usually no contradiction in employing modern medicines alongside traditional remedies with an Islamic base. Here, as in other aspects of their lives, Somalis are staunch pragmatists, valuing what can be shown to produce results. They are quite capable of ridiculing the credulity of those who place an excessive trust in the power of saints or other mystical sources. Men of religion who make excessive demands for alms are in fact often maligned as undeserving beggars to be scorned.

At the same time, mystical power does not hold a complete monopoly in illness and its treatment. Thus there is quite a well-developed traditional lore in bone-setting and minor surgery, including the more hazardous procedure of trepanning. This does not, of course, mean that these and other regularly performed operations such as clitoridectomy and infibulation (regarded as physical techniques for safeguarding virginity before marriage) were carried out with scrupulous attention to hygiene. Serious infections are common, and infertility is a not uncommon result.

Traditional medical lore also included smallpox vaccination, and the isolation of patients with diseases which were known to be infectious. In setting this somewhat patchy indigenous medical practise in perspective, the reader should note that, as the brilliant Oriental scholar and explorer Sir Richard Burton recorded in 1885, Somalis knew from observation of their haunts that mosquitoes carried malaria before this was known to Western science. The success of more recent mass vaccination and innoculation schemes was thus not as unexpected as it might have been if carried out among a population without this traditional knowledge. This demonstrates clearly that the objective assessment of traditional treatments and therapies should be a *sine qua non* before the introduction of new health provisions.

The oral heritage

In the modern world as in the past, Somalis attach great importance to oratory and poetry, which remains in international literary opinion their most significant cultural production, as Richard Burton long ago appreciated (*First Footsteps in East Africa, 1894*—memorial edition). It is here, rather than in the plastic arts that are little developed, that Somalis' most impressive artistic achievements are to be found. This aesthetic specialisation fits well with the nomadic bias of a people used to travelling light with their livestock and few material encumbrances, but a richly compensating gift of language. Somalis are born talkers, poets and story-tellers. Every elder is expected to be able to hold an audience for hours on end with an eloquent speech richly laced with judicious proverbs and quotations from famous poems and sayings. Similarly, if he is to command public respect, he should also be capable not only of composing striking impromptu verse in the various traditional genres, but also of reciting the classic works of famous authors. Since until the mass literacy campaigns of 1972 and 1974 this oral heritage was not preserved in writing, this implied prodigious powers of memory. Indeed it is no exaggeration to say that at their best, traditional elders are walking encyclopedias, with remarkable stores of knowledge based on their life experience and travels.

Although knowledge is primarily local, Somalis are also keenly interested in world news—even if they naturally interpret it somewhat ethnocentrically. They have taken with enthusiasm to radio and television with an insatiable appetite for broadcasts. Similarly there is a growing obsession with the internet where a little literacy goes a long way! By 2007 every major Somali clan and political group had its own website, typically introduced by a 'poem of the day' which further integrated the modern electronic world with the traditional.

The introduction of written Somali, mainly in towns, quickened Somali nationalist feeling associated with the language. Spoken Somali, more than any other single factor, provided the 'open sesame' to Somali society and culture. Although fluency in Somali is a powerful precondition, it does not of course guarantee acceptance; command of Somali potentially gives access to secrets that may be jealously guarded. One of the regular contexts in which men, particularly, are most relaxed is when they meet socially to chew the leaves of the stimulant plant *qat* (*Cathula edulis*) which inspires many dreams (see Cassanelli 1986, pp. 235-60).

Whereas *qat*-chewing sessions were once special (often religious) and occasional pastimes, in the 1980s and 1990s the consumption of the drug, during the day as well as in the evening and individually as well as communally, became pervasive in urban centres such as Mogadishu. After the collapse of the state in 1990/91, young militiamen tended to chew it regularly and were provided with supplies by their leaders. Importing and marketing *qat* from Kenya and Ethiopia became big business in the 1990s and played an important role in the political economy of the 'warlords'. Without abundant supplies of *qat*, male society was apt to grind to a halt, and consumption imposed a heavy burden on the domestic budget.

Self-image and national characteristics

If Somalis appreciate the efforts of foreigners to master their difficult language, their pleasure is tinged with deeply ingrained suspicions. Despite their strong sentiments of national self-esteem and an ethnocentricity which borders on arrogance, they wish to guard the secrets of their culture, and only to share them on their own terms, and as they choose.

The suspicion which greets the stranger is not reserved only for non-Somali foreigners. People of one clan behave in a similar guarded fashion towards those of other, potentially hostile groups. The cautious traditional greeting, 'Is it peace?', shouted at a distance while approaching, is frequently a literal request for information. In the harsh struggle for survival which is the nomad's lot, suspicion is the natural attitude towards those with whom one competes for access to scarce pasture and water. This defence mechanism is extended to all contexts of social interaction and hence becomes a national characteristic.

Since generosity, especially in receiving guests, is also highly valued and a source of pride, the stranger often encounters conflicting attitudes in his hosts. This cautious approach to the outside world, coupled with a politician's skill in seizing the advantage, makes Somalis formidable adversaries. These qualities, particularly among the pastoralists, are combined with aggressive self-confidence and, traditionally, open contempt for other people. This is closely bound up with the nomad's sense of independence and defiant scorn for those who seek to impose their dominion upon him. Displays of superior force are apt to earn only temporary respect as these most ungovernable people bide their time. The reputation they have gained, in their international encounters, for sturdy individualistic independence signals that although they can be reasoned with, they cannot be ordered to do what others want. Connected with this is a certain lack of predictability in routine situations. Somalis are brilliant improvisers and entrepreneurs as, for example, in the modern communications industry. Here their traditional skills in oral communication contribute to their success in establishing internet banking companies which link the remotest nomad to the resources of the modern mercantile world.

These qualities that have so impressed foreigners in their relations with Somalis are somewhat softened among the agricultural Digil Mirifle. Here there is less nonchalant individualism, more respect for authority, a less aggressive welcome, a less suspicious response. This difference in temperament, corresponding to the difference between nomad and farmer, is recognised by both parties and explained in myths which stress the complementarity of both, but the superiority of the nomad.

2

COLONIAL RULE AND INDEPENDENCE: NOMADS AND FARMERS, SOCIALISM AND WAR

The imperial partition (1880–1941)

Although the Somali pastoralists had, traditionally, a strong sense of cultural and linguistic unity, they did not form a single political unit. They were a nation, not a state, although they possessed the cultural prerequisites for statehood. The six major divisions of the nation (the Dir, Isaq, Darod etc.) did not combine together to confront the world, nor did they regularly act as stable or autonomous political units within the Somali political system. They were too large and widely dispersed to do this, and lacked the necessary organisation. They were, in fact, themselves divided into a host of subsidiary clans and clan divisions whose members were frequently widely scattered in their nomadic movements. Throughout the entire nation, these divisions were based primarily on tracing kinship in the male line. At every level, groups were formed on the basis of descent traced in this way from common ancestors. Hence family genealogies provided the basic structure of group division and political identity. Of course, the reasons for division or unity depended on interests, as perceived, at different points in time, e.g. competition over grazing or water, commercial control in towns etc.

Clans and their lineage divisions were led by 'the elders'—in principle all senior, adult men. The most stable unit in a flexible and shifting pattern of alignments was the '*diya*-paying group'. This consisted, usually, of a few hundred male heads of closely related families who were parties to a joint treaty or contract (*her*) to pay and receive compensation for injuries or death or, in default, seek revenge. Some clans had institutionalised positions of clan heads, but in general this was a republican society, without the chiefs found so widely elsewhere in Africa.

These divisions within the otherwise generally homogeneous Somali national culture facilitated the imperial partition of this region during the scramble for Africa. In the closing decades of the nineteenth century, the two superpowers competing in the region were the British and the French. Their primary interest centred on control of the Nile waters. The British were installed at Aden and sought to prevent, or minimize, French influence on the adjacent Somali coast. They used their allies, the Italians, as an additional means of countering French ambitions. The French had a somewhat similar relationship with the Russians, who at this time, had a lively interest in the Horn of Africa. To safeguard the supply of Somali mutton for the Aden garrison, in the 1880s the British signed 'protection' treaties with a number of northern Somali clans. The French and the Italians did likewise. During the revolt against Anglo-Egyptian rule in the Sudan led by the Sudanese Mahdi, the French, Russians and Italians poured arms into Ethiopia. Russia and Italy were competing to make Ethiopia a client state.

These aspirations were dashed at the battle of Adowa in 1896 when the Ethiopians used their new weapons to rout an Italian army based in the expanding Italian colony of Eritrea. Having already seized the Muslim citadel of Harar in 1884 (visited by

Burton in 1856) Menelik was now firmly installed as Emperor of Ethiopia and engaged on a policy of imperial expansion and aggrandisement. Britain, France, Russia and Italy were soon forced to recognise that Ethiopia was the local superpower (as it still was in 2007) and had to trim their ambitions accordingly. Russia, at this point, effectively withdrew, leaving arms and some military advisers behind. Britain, France and Italy negotiated with Menelik whose armies were now seeking to impose Ethiopian (i.e. Amhara, the ruling ethnic group) dominion over Cushitic-speaking Oromo and Somali peoples round Harar and to the southeast.

In this process, the Somali nation was divided into five parts. That based on Djibouti which, with the construction of the Franco-Ethiopian railway to Addis Ababa, became Ethiopia's main port, was under French rule and included ethnically related Afar tribesmen. Next came the British Somaliland Protectorate which had Hargeisa as its main town, and its neighbour, Italian Somalia, with Mogadishu as its capital. Other Somalis eventually came under the British flag in northern Kenya. Finally, the fifth division consisted of that large area known after its main Somali residents as the Ogaden, and the Somali territory around Dire Dawa (Dire Dabbe in Somali). This was the Ethiopian portion, although Ethiopian jurisdiction was not at the time unambiguously acknowledged by Britain or Italy—partly because recognition of Ethiopian title to the area was in conflict with prior Anglo-Somali treaties and because Italy retained wider aspirations. These five divisions of the nation are represented in the five-pointed Somali star, the national emblem adopted by the Somali Republic at the time of independence in 1960.

This partition and the encroachment by Christian colonisers provoked a violent reaction. The fiery Ogaden religious leader Sayyid Muhammad Abdille Hassan and his Dervish forces mounted their protracted guerrilla campaign to drive the 'infidel' usurpers out of Somali territory and to regain Somali independence. Significantly, the first major engagement, against the

Ethiopians, took place at Jigjiga. When in 1920 this 'holy war' finally collapsed and Sayyid Muhammad died, all the colonial powers were more deeply entrenched than before. The British had been forced to assume control of the hinterland, and not merely of the coast as they had intended originally, and the Italians were consolidating their colony of Somalia in which they were encouraging Italian settlers to develop fruit plantations. Recruiting local labour, often of ex-slave origin, in the fertile inter-riverine areas of southern Somalia, Italian settlers introduced new commercial crops, including bananas which were exported to Italy by Italian companies under a monopoly arrangement. Outside Mogadishu, the country was administered by expatriate Italian District and Provincial Commissioners in much the same fashion as Somaliland was administered by Britain, and at a local level through local leaders recognised by the Italians as 'chiefs' (referred to by the curious Italo-Arabic hybrid '*capo-qabilah*') who, where they cooperated readily with the authorities, were lavishly rewarded with colonial medals and minor titles. This pattern of 'indirect rule' was on the whole more developed than under the British. Fascism, as it gathered momentum in Italy, was implemented locally by strongly differentiating the 'natives' from their 'natural rulers', the Italian colonisers.

Somaliland, Britain's 'Cinderella of Empire', where there were no European settlers in contrast to the thousands of Italians in fascist Somalia, remained an essentially Somali territory very different from cosmopolitan Somalia. Although comparisons were made by administrators with developments in the British Sudan after the defeat of the Mahdi there, there were no comparable advances, economic or social, after the fall of Sayyid Muhammad Abdille Hassan. Attempts were made to expand education and even to introduce a script to enable Somali to become a written language, but these were strongly, indeed violently opposed at the time by the conservative population of the Protectorate. While the ban on Christian missionary activity was closely observed, such were public sensitivities and suspicions that it was only in 1938 that the first government school was opened, and not until the 1950s that schooling for girls was introduced. From its beginnings, Western education in Somaliland remained small-scale and elitist in its selection of pupils.

In Somalia a wider level of education with a more varied curriculum, though generally of a lower standard, was instituted by the Italians, and mission activity (usually associated with medical clinics and care of orphans) was not totally excluded: there were indeed soon enough Christian Somalis to attend regular masses with the Italian settlers, and eventually even a Catholic cathedral (destroyed by bomb blasts just before the collapse of the Mogadishu government in 1990/91).

This local religious tolerance in the 1930s did not prevent growing friction between the Italians and Ethiopians over the frontier between their respective territories, which were never definitively demarcated. Such lack of precise territorial definition was encouraged by Italy's prolonged thrust to gain control of Ethiopia, and by Ethiopia's own expansionist designs. This conflict was brought to a flashpoint by a confrontation in 1934 between soldiers of the two sides at the oasis of Walwal in the eastern Somali Ogaden, and this provided the pretext the Italians sought for their long-prepared invasion of the Ethiopian highlands, which prompted mounting international concern. Thus what proved to be one of the most unexpected paths to the Second World War originated in the remote Ogaden desert. The ensuing fascist conquest of Ethiopia, employing air raids with poison gas, was completed a year later and, in the early phases of the World War, the Italians drove the British out of their Somaliland Protectorate, setting up their short-lived 'Italian African Empire' with its capital in Addis Ababa. Both the Italians and the British had Somali recruits in their forces, and a strong rapport sprang up, especially in Somalia, between Somalis and the liberating British troops who defeated the Italians in 1941. This was reflected in the ethos of the British

Military Administration (BMA) which then took over control of all the Somali territories except Djibouti. The BMA was staffed by imaginative and innovative individuals, of many diverse backgrounds prior to their military service, who took their responsibility of training Somali recruits seriously and emphasised useful skills as well as general education. The reformed police force (now called the Somali gendarmerie) looked to the future with the promotion of Somalis to positions of leadership. Thus Muhammad Abshir, a young officer recruit in the early 1940s, commanded the force at independence in 1960, and a rival colleague, Muhammad Siyad Barre, rose to be head of state in the coup which militarised Somalia and eventually led to its collapse.

The re-partition of the Somalis (1941–60)

After the defeat of the Italians by the Allies in 1941, with the exception of Djibouti the whole Somali region came under British military rule. In the subsequent 'Big Four Power' (Britain, France, USA and the USSR) negotiations on the future status of the ex-Italian colonies, Britain originally proposed the formation of a united Somali state under UN Trusteeship and British administration, although British administration was not insisted on. This proposal, however, was rejected, and the Somali nation again partitioned. The British Somaliland Protectorate was reinstated and the Italians returned in 1950 to administer their former colony of Somalia for a period of ten years under UN Trusteeship. The Ogaden and adjacent Somali territories, despite vigorous protests by their inhabitants, were gradually returned to Ethiopian rule. Somali nationalist political parties, encouraged by the benevolent paternalism of British military rule in Somalia from 1941 to 1950, were now vigorously active: indeed the Somali Youth League, the first major nationalist organ, was created in Mogadishu in its original form with BMA encouragement. Self-determination in the Somali area of eastern Ethiopia ('Western Somalia') was already an acute issue and had BMA support. The Colonial Office took on this pro-Somali mantle while the Foreign Office favoured Ethiopia, an interesting example of the complexity of colonial policies and their implementation. Although an attempt was made to buy back the Haud region of the Ogaden from Ethiopia, when this did not succeed Ethiopian interests won the day.

Ethiopia was thus doubly compensated for the fascist conquest. With Haile Selassie reinstalled on his throne, Ethiopia was given both the Ogaden and neighbouring Somali areas and the former Italian colony of Eritrea. Eritrea was initially federated with Ethiopia in 1952, but a decade later was annexed as simply another province of Haile Selassie's empire. This action led to the formation of the Eritrean separatist movements and their guerrilla struggle, which was to become a landmark liberation struggle and one of the longest on the continent, ending when Eritrea became independent in 1993.

Independence 1960–69

Following the desires expressed by the political leaders in both countries, British Somaliland was hastily prepared for independence so that it could join with Somalia when the latter became independent in 1960. In the event the British Protectorate became self-governing on 26 June, and on 1 July 1960 joined Italian Somalia to form the Somali Republic under a government formed from those then in power in the two territories. The two legislatures met in joint session in Mogadishu, and formally joined to form the new republic's national assembly, electing the former assembly president, Adan Abdulle Osman (Hawiye), as provisional president of the state. The more complex business of composing the cabinet of the new government took a little time. After two weeks of delicate negotiation the Prime Minister, Dr Abdirashid Ali Shermarke (Darod), who had studied political science in Italy, announced his 14 cabinet colleagues. These represented all the

33

parties in the north and south and all the major clan groupings, closely replicating the ratio of northern (33) and southern (90) seats in the assembly. The Somaliland Prime Minister, Mohamed Haji Ibrahim Egal, became minister of Defence, while Abdillahi Ise, who had stepped aside to make room for Abdirashid, was appointed foreign minister.

Although the UN 'experiment' in Somalia had worked in the simple sense of providing a European-style centralised state framework and a corresponding administrative organisation, no serious thought had been given to considering how appropriate these would prove in the local setting, or above all in conjunction with the highly decentralised nature of traditional Somali political institutions. This was an entirely Eurocentric exercise which assumed that all cases of self-determination were essentially the same and posed the same problems. It is easier, of course, to appreciate these issues in retrospect after the collapse of Somalia and failure of every effort to resurrect a functioning state. As we shall see, there is still no sign that national and international authorities grasp the problem posed by Somali traditional politics. This gulf in comprehension is not helped by the fact that Somalis themselves tend to minimise these crucial differences in political organisation.

The post-independence problems perceived by Somali politicians and UN and European mandarins alike were primarily economic and resource based. These were to a large extent to be solved, in the short term at least, by aid to develop Somalia's scarce resources. Also requiring attention, of course, was the gap between the British and Italian colonial traditions. This was a major preoccupation during the first few years of independence. Apart from the obvious language problem which pervaded all spheres of activity, there were wide divergencies between Italian and British practice in administration, bureaucratic procedure, accounting, law etc. These were not easily resolved and there was often considerable friction between British- and Italian-trained personnel.

Trouble was forecast when on 20 June 1961 a referendum was held to approve the provisional constitution under which the two ex-colonial territories had united at independence. Of the mere 100,000 in the north who voted on this issue half rejected the constitution, whereas in the south it was strongly supported. Thus at least half of the northerners rejected the union of the two halves of the republic a year after it had been formed. A more ominous signal of discontent was the abortive northern officers' coup of 1961. Nevertheless, although a simmering resentment remained, by the mid-60s a considerable degree of effective integration had in fact been achieved, both in politics and in administration. The leaders of the political parties had evidently come to accept the Somali Republic as an established fact, and readjusted their alignments correspondingly. But had their publics fully accommodated to this new situation?

This awkward and uneven process was in some respects eased by the majority position enjoyed by the major party, the Somali Youth League (founded in 1943), and more importantly by the ties of kinship binding elected members of the National Assembly to their rural constituents. While nationalist leaders generally sought to eradicate these internal clan divisions within the nation, they continued to exert a pervasive influence on all aspects of life. The persistent power of traditional loyalties, leading to the preferment of individuals irrespective of their qualifications, made it very difficult for the bureaucracy to function effectively. In a nationalistic atmosphere hostile to those retrograde forces, it became fashionable to refer to clan divisions indirectly rather than directly. In place of their clans people began to speak of 'ex-clans', and the word 'ex' was adopted into Somali with this sense. Thus, by an adroit trick of language, the problems of clan divisions were ostensibly resolved by consigning them to history and talking about them in the past tense as though they had ceased to exist. This, of course, was not at all the case.

The pan-Somali struggle (1960–69)

While modest developments were being pursued internally with the help of foreign aid, mainly from Western countries, Somali foreign policy was dominated by the Somali unification issue. The Somali Republic founded on the premise of Somali national identity was an incomplete state. It did not contain a whole nation, three parts of which remained under foreign rule in Ethiopia, Djibouti and northern Kenya. The main initial thrust to overcome this issue was directed towards Kenya. Prior to Kenyan independence, negotiations with Britain sought to gain autonomy, separate from Kenya, for the northern Somali districts. When, under pressure from Kenya's nationalist leaders, Britain disregarded the report of an official British Commission to assess Somali aspirations in the area, the Somali Republic broke off diplomatic relations with the United Kingdom. This rebuff caused great resentment among the Somali population of northern Kenya and led to the Somali guerrilla campaign (known to the Kenyan authorities as the 'shifta' or bandit war) which paralysed the region from 1963 to 1967.

It was natural to focus the Pan-Somali self-determination issue primarily on the Somali community in northern Kenya in the run-up to Kenyan independence. But it was not possible to ignore Somali aspirations elsewhere. The creation of the Somali Republic inevitably encouraged nationalist sentiment in the Ogaden, and incidents between Somali nomads and the Ethiopian military authorities became increasingly frequent. Despite UN and Italian efforts in the period from 1950 to 1960 to reach agreement on the definition of the boundary between Somalia and Ethiopia, there was still no generally agreed frontier between the two states. The line shown on the map was still the provisional administrative line used during the British Military Administration of the area.

At the end of 1963 a Somali uprising in the Ogaden led to a brief major confrontation between the Ethiopian and Somalian armed forces. With pan-Somali nationalism exerting such an influence and with American and Western military support for Ethiopia and Kenya, it was natural that the Somali Republic should reject an offer of limited defensive arms from the West in favour of a more generous and open-ended Soviet arms commitment. This Russian military connection, which did not at the time lead Somalia to move far from its neutralist but generally pro-Western stance, was to have far-reaching effects later.

The new civilian government formed in June 1967 under the premiership of Mohamed Haji Ibrahim Egal (Isaq), a northerner from the former British Protectorate, and with Abdirashid Ali Shermarke as President led to a marked shift in Somali foreign policy. Concluding that the aggressive pursuit of the pan-Somali struggle favoured by previous governments had yielded little positive return, Egal embarked on a policy of détente with Kenya and Ethiopia, seeking to gain a new understanding with the leaders of both countries as a basis for more fruitful negotiation.

This development, thrusting the Pan-Somali issue temporarily into the background, was one of many factors that contributed to the eventual downfall of Prime Minister Egal and his replacement by military rule. What turned out to be Somalia's last civilian elections were held in March 1969, when 1,002 candidates representing 62 parties (mainly thinly disguised clan organisations) competed for 123 seats in the National Assembly. The Somali Youth League victory turned into a landslide when all the 'independent' members of the Assembly, with one exception, joined the government party, led by Egal and President Shermarke. In the usual African one-party style, Somalia now came under increasingly autocratic rule, with Egal's government paying little attention to the dissent provoked by its growing autocracy. The unexpected assassination of the President on 15 October 1969, by a disaffected member of his bodyguard, administered a sharp jolt and was followed on 21

October by a well-staged military coup in which the army calmly seized power without encountering opposition.

Military rule and revolution (1969–74)

The original impetus for the coup came from a group of young army officers impatient, as they proclaimed, with the corruption, nepotism and inefficiency of Egal's government. But it soon became clear that the new Head of State and President of the Supreme Revolutionary Council (SRC), General Muhammad Siyad Barre, Commander of the Army, held the reins of power firmly in his hands. General Siyad, who like his personal rival the popular former police commander General Mohamed Abshir (now placed in detention) had been a police inspector during the British Military Administration, had also trained in Italy where he had privately studied politics. Assisted by a council of largely civilian, technocratic-style secretaries of state, the SRC—with its 25 members drawn from the army and police, ranging in rank from general to captain—embarked on an energetic policy of internal administrative reform. The aim, which was popular initially, was to clean out the Augean stables and restore Somali virtues with a concerted onslaught, under energetic leadership, on the real enemies of progress: poverty, disease and ignorance.

Reform and galvanisation of the nation's energies were pursued by a battery of new measures. Civilian district and provincial governors were replaced by military personnel who were installed as chairmen of local revolutionary councils modelled on that in Mogadishu. Unemployed urban tribal drop-outs were recruited for a whole series of public work projects. The death sentence was reintroduced to replace blood compensation (*diya*) paid traditionally in inter-clan feuds. This was part of a wider strategy aimed at abolishing traditional clan divisions and so strengthening the 'nation'.

Scientific Socialism in Somalia

These policies acquired a more distinctive ideological edge with the official adoption of Scientific Socialism (in Somali, literally 'wealth-sharing based on knowledge') on the first anniversary of the coup in October 1970. The coup had now become retrospectively a 'bloodless revolution'. This change of direction reflected the army's growing dependence on Russia and the idealistic orientation of young intellectuals unimpressed by Somalia's previous pro-Western policies. This development was coupled with national campaigns and 'crash programmes' against corruption and tribalism, effigies representing those anachronistic 'impediments to progress' being burnt at official ceremonies early in 1971. The word *jalle*—literally comrade, or friend—was officially launched as the approved term of greeting and address to replace the traditional terms 'uncle' and 'cousin', with their unacceptable clan allusions. Locally based people's vigilantes, called the 'victory leaders' (*guulwadayal)*, frequently recruited from the unemployed, were organised to lead community development projects. Destitute children and orphaned street boys were similarly gathered into Revolutionary Youth Centres where they were clothed, fed and educated in the new revolutionary ideals. At a national level the same values were instilled, along with military training, at the former military academy in Mogadishu, renamed 'Halane' after a Somali lieutenant who had died in the 1964 Somali-Ethiopian fighting while attempting to save his country's colours.

At the same time, under the diligent direction of the Ministry of Information and National Guidance, a national cult, amalgamating Chinese, North Korean and Nasserite as well as Soviet influence, was created around the Head of State as benevolent 'Father' of a nation whose 'Mother' was the 'Glorious Revolution'. This cult of the President was accompanied by the publication of pithy extracts from his speeches and sayings (e.g. 'less talk and more work') and in radio programmes which ingeniously blended these and Marxist themes with Islamic motifs; he was widely known by his nickname '*Af-weyne*' (literally, 'big mouth') which he sometimes used himself. The political office of the Presidency was expanded into a national organisation of *apparatchik*s staffing local orientation centres, established in all main settlements. The walls of these, in common with public posters, featured the new ruling trinity of *Jalle* Markis (Marx), *Jalle* Lenin and *Jalle* Siyad. Revolutionary vigilance was maintained by the National Security Service (NSS: headed by Siyad's Darod/Dulbahante son-in-law, 'Dufleh'), with arbitrary powers of arrest and detention, and the National Security Courts which, dispensing with legal safeguards on individual liberty, dealt out a rough justice.

In a further effort to reduce the continuing influence of clan ties—acknowledged in a number of the President's bitter harangues—the eight provinces of the Republic were reconstituted as 15 new regions, comprising 78 districts, renamed where necessary to exclude clan names: for example, Mijerteinia became Bari. Stress was placed on the local settlement as a basic unit of identification in place of clan allegiance, and marriages, traditionally inter-clan affairs, were to be celebrated in Orientation Centres and stripped of clan significance. In the same spirit the former lineage and clan heads ('chiefs' and elders) were renamed 'peace-seekers' and theoretically transformed into part of the state bureaucracy.

This assault on the traditional structure of society in an effort to secure modernisation was coupled with a policy of state control of the economy. The export of the banana crop grown in the riverine areas south of Mogadishu was controlled by a state agency not greatly different from the monopoly established by previous civilian governments. Similarly grain production was controlled, farmers being allowed to keep a small quantity of grain for their own use and obliged to sell the rest at fixed prices to the Agricultural Development Corporation which stored it and arranged for its distribution and sale to the public. Imported goods were similarly regulated through a state agency. The major local industries, the sugar factory at Jowhar and the meat processing plant at Kismayu, were likewise state enterprises.

This impressive apparatus of state machinery was, however, only part of the picture. The mainstay of the country's economy remained the pastoral sector from which livestock, Somalia's main product, were exported on the hoof to the Arab markets by private enterprise, although hides and skins were mainly exported via a government agency. Private import/export companies and construction firms continued to pursue a lucrative trade, and on a smaller scale, small urban businesses and shops followed these old patterns of free enterprise, sometimes under new, socialist sounding names.

The Supreme Revolutionary Council's revolutionary aims were most directly pursued through national 'crash programmes' launched by the President with full military honours. The most impressive of these were undoubtedly the urban and rural mass literacy campaigns of 1973 and 1974. Previous civilian governments had never had the courage to decide on and implement a script for the national language. The issue was indeed controversial with public opinion divided between supporters of Arabic, the Latin script, and various Somali-invented scripts. President Siyad's regime sensibly adopted the Latin script, which was the most suitable medium, and proceeded to encourage mass literacy. In the 1973 urban campaign, officials were given intensive courses which they had to pass at reasonable levels if they wished to retain their positions. Voluntary adult literacy classes proved popular and successful.

The following year the scheme, enlarged to include health and veterinary components, was extended to the rural and largely nomadic population through a nation-wide Campaign for Rural Development, employing some 30,000 secondary school students and their teachers. Unfortunately, this programme turned out to coincide with one of the worst droughts in Somali history, in which a quarter of a million nomads lost most of their livestock and had to be supported in relief camps and later grouped in agricultural and fishing settlements, mainly in southern Somalia. In this humane response to a national calamity, the government seized the opportunity of promoting its long-term aims of curtailing nomadism and attempting to inculcate the new revolutionary ideals among the refractory nomadic population. To those who criticised these ideals for not being those of orthodox Marxism, the response, formulated by a young Somali intellectual in a debate with a well-known Marxist French anthropologist, was, 'We don't need Marx, Marx needs us!' Later events did not fully confirm this bold assertion.

The resumption of the pan-Somali struggle (1974-78)

The first phase of General Siyad Barre's rule (1969-74) was one of concentration on internal problems: local development and consolidation of the regime's authority. 1974 marked the inauguration of a new expansive phase. In that year Somalia joined the Arab League, thereby gaining some leverage with Russia, and also hosted and chaired the Organisation of African Unity Heads of State meeting. Although joining the Arab League evoked merriment in some Somali circles, this new prominence invited a more thrusting policy on the pan-Somali issue, to which added piquancy was inevitably given by the increasing paralysis of Ethiopia in the wake of Haile Selassie's overthrow in September 1974. Somalia's military rulers had introduced the customary anti-imperialist rhetoric (refreshingly unstressed in Somalia prior to 1969) and this was now mainly directed towards France, in relation to Djibouti, and Ethiopia. African support here was, naturally, mainly restricted to the Djibouti self-determination issue. Especially because of the sensitivity of African frontiers, it was difficult for African governments to rally to Somalia's side in its denunciation of Ethiopian imperialism which, being black, hardly counted.

The pace of events in Djibouti progressed with surprising speed, reaching a somewhat unexpected conclusion in June 1977 when the territory became independent under a Somali president (see Lewis 2002, pp. 228-31). To summarise briefly, the territory had swung from Afar domination back to an uneasy Somali-Afar alliance, under Somali leadership, bolstered by French and Arab support. This outcome was something for which the architects of Somalia's external policies could take some credit.

The Somali government was, now, however, under very heavy pressure from its co-nationals and their allies in Ethiopia. In the wake of the early Ogaden insurgency of 1960-64 a similar but more recalcitrant guerrilla movement had arisen among the Muslim (Arussi) Oromo in Bale Province. Having finally made peace with Haile Selassie in 1970 and received a traditional Ethiopian title, the leader of this rising, Wako Goto, followed many of his kinsmen in seeking asylum in Somalia. These and other anti-Amhara dissidents from the Ogaden were constantly pressing the Somali government to come to their aid in a concerted liberation struggle against their Ethiopian rulers. The Ogaden nationalists had already set up their widely appealing Western Somali Liberation Front (WSLF), which was allied to the Bale insurgents who became active again in 1975-76. By the spring of 1977, Oromo guerrilla forces had recovered control of most of the countryside in Bale and in the north the war in Eritrea had reached a critical phase, with the local nationalists controlling most of the region and pressing heavily on the beleaguered and demoralised Ethiopian garrisons in Asmara and Massawa.

As the new military leaders in Ethiopia increasingly proclaimed their dedication to revolutionary socialism, the urgency of finding a solution for Somali nationalism in eastern Ethiopia (or 'Western Somalia') was reflected in a Russo-Cuban venture which brought Fidel Castro to the region in March 1977 to mediate between Colonel Mengistu and General Siyad. This underlined the Russian interest in Ethiopia, which increased as Ethiopia's relations with its traditional patron, the USA, deteriorated, party as a consequence of the Carter administration's reluctance to continue

43

to supply arms which would be applied to suppress the Eritrean nationalists (America, in addition, had acquired the Diego Garcia base in the Indian Ocean and could, presumably, afford to dispense with the older strategic base at Kagnew in Eritrea).

Mengistu's visit to Moscow in May seemed to set the seal on the seismic shift of superpower allegiances in the area and was the final precipitant leading to the war in Eastern Ethiopia/Western Somalia. The Western Somali Liberation Front, or their allies, began their military campaign to expel the Ethiopians from Somali ethnic territory by cutting the strategically significant line of rail between Addis Ababa and Djibouti on the eve of the latter's independence.

With tacit and cautious support from the Mogadishu government, the WSLF launched the whirlwind advance which, by late September 1977, brought its forces to the gates of Harar in the wake of the retreat by the demoralised Ethiopian forces. Russia now rallied to Ethiopia's defence, mounting a massive airlift of sophisticated military equipment with Russian and East German military advisers and Cuban and South Yemeni combat troops. Inevitably Somali-Soviet relations rapidly deteriorated. The anticipated breach occurred on 13 November, less than a month after the successful rescue of the passengers aboard a hijacked Lufthansa jet at Mogadishu airport, which opened the door to an unprecedented influx of Western aid.

The Russian exodus from Somalia and the victories in the Ogaden led to immense elation, and greatly increased the popularity of the Siyad regime. The terrible debacle which followed in the spring of 1978 when, with Russo-Cuban support and greatly superior firepower, the Ethiopians reimposed their rule in Western Somalia, inevitably shook the Somali government to its foundations.

Although the Somalis had understood the United States as indicating willingness to replace Russia as Somalia's patron superpower, this had not actually happened. For the time being, because of the sensitivity of the question of the frontiers of African states, American and indeed Western aid generally seemed restricted to civilian projects. This left a yawning gulf exacerbating internal sources of instability—all greatly increased since the Ogaden War and its outcome. The delicacy of the political situation was shown most obviously in Somalia by the abortive military coup of April 1978, which far from 'clearing the air' in the Republic, left things as confused and uncertain as ever. The regime's survival, though by no means assured, was encouraged, in the short term at least, by the divisions among those who opposed it.

The Russian legacy

The enthusiasm with which the public greeted the Russian departure in part reflected the way in which the Russians were generally identified with the more oppressive aspects of the Siyad government, particularly the National Security Service and the National Security Courts. In the summer of 1978 there was some evidence that, without their Russian and East German advisers, those organisations were considered to be less arbitrary in their activities and less threatening to ordinary people. Whether or not this reflected also a deliberate policy decision at the centre of power, or a weakening of the centre's hold (suggested by other factors), was hard to assess. Those who so wished could find some support for the former interpretation in the announcement on the ninth anniversary of the Revolution, in October 1978, that there would be a constitution and a return to parliamentary rule. It was announced that some 3,000 prisoners (presumably some held for political reasons) would be released. But a few days later, the 17 people who had been found guilty of leading the April coup were publicly executed by firing squad.

The Constitution and 'people's parliament' established in 1979 in the spirit of 'democratic centralism' clearly provided new scope for the official Somali Revolutionary Socialist Party formed, under Soviet pressure, in June 1976. This organisation, with an official membership of just over 12,000 in 1977, the majority classed as 'workers and employees' and 735 as 'peasants', was a direct out-growth of the earlier Political Office of the Presidency which it replaced. The Party was directed by a Supreme Council with 73 members, one a woman.

The Central Committee of the Party, incorporating members of the former Supreme Revolutionary Council, was divided into 19 departments, each headed by a Committee member, and linked with the various government ministries and state agencies. All government ministers, with the exception of the Transport minister, were members of the Central Committee. The vital Political Bureau, the real seat of authority and power, was led by the President of the Republic and Chairman of the Party, General Siyad, aided by three Vice-Presidents (the Minister of Defence, the Assistant to the President for Presidential Affairs, and the Assistant to the Chairman for Party Affairs) and by the Head of the National Security Service.

If these developments appeared to provide a more representative government in which the younger civilian intellectuals had a more formalised position, there was no question as to the ultimate source of power. Indeed, in the wake of the Ogaden defeat and the rupture with Russia it appeared, as might have been anticipated, that the President was consolidating his position on traditionalist lines. Despite all his rhetoric directed against tribalism and clan ties, members of the public tended to regard President Siyad's regime as based primarily on three main traditional divisions of the Darod clan confederacy. These were his own clan, the Marrehan, based on the middle Juba; his mother's clan, the Ogaden; and that of his son-in-law and head of the National Security Service, the Dulbahante. The last-named straddled the border between the former British Somaliland Protectorate and Italian Somalia and hence acted as a highly significant lynchpin in the structure of the united Republic.

This configuration of family ties, summed up in the clandestine nickname 'MOD', proved a powerful formula for rule in the Somali Democratic Republic. The practical implication was that, in relation to their numbers, these three groups were over-represented in key positions throughout the state. Otherwise, comparison of the composition of successive Somali governments shows that General Siyad's regime contained members of all the major clan groups on the established, if disavowed, principle of clan representation.

The regime's power-base was significantly widened by the opening of the 'people's parliament', with 171 elected members (all belonging to the SRS Party), at the end of December 1979. President Siyad reshuffled his cabinet and abolished the titles, if not the roles, of his three Vice-Presidents. With the refugee crisis (*see below*) aggravated by lack of fuel supplies, in October 1980 the President felt it necessary to declare a state of emergency and resurrected the Supreme Revolutionary Council. He thus sought to regain firm control of an increasingly difficult situation and to combat public corruption and inefficiency. His own practices were, of course, another matter. Confronted by mounting insecurity, internally and externally, it was natural that the regime should attempt to retrench itself with all the means at its disposal. These included the formal power structure developed in the first years of the Revolution and the more traditional clan ties.

Thus, as nationalism and Islam counted for far more than ideology in foreign policy, so at home traditional forces continued to play a decisive role in politics, whatever the official picture which, after the breach with Russia, continued to stress dedication to Socialism, with perhaps less emphasis on the qualifying adjective 'scientific'. Cynical Somali commentators observed that the Socialist path provided a convenient formula for autocracy. It seemed likely, however, that there might be easing of the tension between Socialism and traditionalist Islam, of which the most violent instance had been the execution in January 1975 of ten religious leaders who had attacked liberal new measures designed to give women equal inheritance rights with men.

Government and rural society

The governmental reorganisation associated with the establish-ment of the Party had significant implications for the adminis-tration of the country as a whole. The Ministry of the Interior which had formerly controlled the Police Force was disbanded, its functions being parcelled out between the Presidency, the Party, the Ministry of Local Government and Rural Development, and such state agencies as the Resettlement Agency, the Cooperatives Board, and the Agricultural Crash Programme. Just as formerly the Central SRC structure had been replicated at regional and district level by corresponding local Councils, so now the regional and district administrative units came under the authority of cor-responding Party Committees. Thus the role of Regional Gover-nor merged with District Secretary, the resulting key official being aided by a First Assistant for Party Affairs and a Second Assistant for Administrative Affairs. The appointment and operation of these local administrative officials was overseen and coordinated by a Regional Inspectorate of high-ranking officials (several of them military officers) reporting to the President, formally via the Vice-President and Presidential Affairs Assistant, General Hus-seyn Kulmiye (a former minister of the Interior).

Despite these elaborate changes in nomenclature, there was much continuity between the 1980s regional power structure and the earlier organisation based on Revolutionary Councils. Re-gional and district governors were still closely controlled by the Presidency, their actions being subject to the vigilant scrutiny of the local heads of the National Security Service (NSS) and but-tressed by the local police and army commanders. While some regional and district headquarters could muster small associations of workers with whom to discuss local issues, the main linkage between this official state apparatus and the bulk of the rural population was through the local clan elders. These established traditional figures had been officially known since the Revolution as 'peace seekers' (*nabad-don*) and were supposed to act as intermediaries between their clansmen and the official authorities. Local religious leaders (sheikhs, in Somali *wadad*) played a similar consultative role, at least in theory.

Traditional rural social institutions

The most pervasive organisational principle in traditional Somali social organisation is kinship, traced patrilineally in the male line. Genealogies tracing descent (*tol*) from common ancestors are the basis for the division of the population into clan and sub-clan. Despite the effects of increasing monetarisation of the traditional economy, official measures designed to eradicate clan loyalties, and other forces for change, these ties continued to provide the individual's primary identity within the Somali nation. The kinship unit with which the individual identified was always relative and varied according to the situation in which allegiance was evoked. For instance, people of Darod descent so identify themselves in opposition to Isaq, Hawiye, Dir, Digil and Rahanweyn. Within Darod, the further divisions of Ogaden, Mijerteyn, Marrehan, Dulbahante and other clans become relevant. Each of these clans comprises hundreds of sub-groups. These kinship ties are traced backwards through the individual's father, his father's father, the latter's father and so on until the founding ancestor (Darod, Isaq etc.) is reached. The 'number of generations counted apart', as Somalis put it, provides a ready-reckoner of closeness or remoteness in people's relations with each other. The term 'cousin' (or, in the case of a younger man addressing an older man, 'uncle') is applied to all those other than brothers who share recognised common descent. The word 'cousin' or 'uncle' is also applied as a polite term of address when speaking to an unrelated stranger.

The term *jalle*—friend, or comrade—introduced by the Siyad regime sought to replace this traditional usage and its associated and potentially divisive kinship connotations. Although ostentatiously employed by ministers and senior officials of the regime, *jalle* was not widely used by ordinary citizens.

Ties with the mother's brother's clan (for example, between President Siyad's Marrehan and the Ogaden) are also extremely important. They have, in principle, a warm friendly character and may be used to supplement the axiomatic solidarity based on patrilineal kinship (*tol*). The mother's brother's group is known as *Rer Abti*, *'rer'* being the most general term for 'group' or 'people' and *abti* the term for mother's brother. Ties established by marriage (*hidid*) are also significant, especially where—as is generally the case among the northern Somali nomads—marriage is an alliance contracted between potentially hostile groups.

If patrilineal kinship is the primary bond, it creates diffuse loyalties that are given specific focus by a contractual treaty (*her*) defining the limits of solidarity in blood vengeance. The payment and receipt of blood compensation (*diya* in Arabic, *mag* in Somali)—or, in default, the duty to pursue vengeance—falls on a restricted group of closely related kin who accept this as a collective obligation. Such compensation agreements detailing the way in which a particular group of kin would protect the life and property of their members were, during the colonial period, lodged in District Office headquarters, and *diya*-paying groups formed on this basis behaved and were treated as the primary political divisions of the population (for a full analysis see Lewis, *A Pastoral Democracy*, 1999; see also Mohamed Jama 2007*)*.

Although official policy after independence, and especially after the 1969 Revolution, sought to undermine these traditional arrangements, they still persisted in a less formalised fashion. Death by firing squad as the penalty for apprehended murderers during the 'revolutionary' period appeared to result in traditional feud being less common than it once was. However, it was not eradicated, and collective claims for blood compensation were still advanced even in such contexts as urban traffic accidents;

blood-money was even said to have been paid out by an insurance company.

It was very much in terms of these traditional patterns of clan vengeance that people in the summer of 1978 were discussing the execution of the mainly Mijerteyn leaders of the abortive April coup. This was seen by many as a feud between the Mijerteyn and the President's Marrehan clan (both Darod)—an intepretation which, in the view of some Somali commentators, enabled the President to distract attention from wider discontents shared by members of other clans.

At all levels of grouping, policy is traditionally decided by the elders (*odayal*, singular *oday*—the word *duk* is also used, and *akhyar* in southern Somalia). Some clans also have dynastic families of clan heads, sometimes called 'Sultans' (also known as *Ugas, Garad, Boqor* etc.), a role which is, on the whole, more defined among the southern agricultural Digil and Rahanweyn Somali, living between the Shebelle and Juba rivers. These southern farming Somalis have traditionally had leaders with a more authoritative position than is generally the case among pastoral nomads (see Helander 2003). Before they were all renamed 'peace-seekers' (*nabad-don*) by the revolutionary government, the Digil and Rahanweyn clan leaders were usually known distinctively by the colloquial Italian-Arabic title '*capo-qabila*' (the Arabic word *qabila* is sometimes applied in Somali to clans).

Local groups and settlement patterns

As is to be expected, the pastoral nomads who make up the bulk of the population have a much more fluid and flexible pattern of distribution than the cultivators. The pastoralist units here called 'clans' (Dulbahante, Habar Toljalo, Marrehan etc.) had and continue to have loosely defined areas of movement. Their most clearly defined bases are the dry season wells customarily used for watering camels when water is scarce. It is usually at such wa-

51

tering places that market and administrative centres have grown up. While among the northern nomads, at this level of grouping, there are roughly established 'spheres of influence', there are also many areas in which different groups regularly graze their stock, and rhythmic seasonal patterns of movement dependent on the distribution of rain, pasture and water. So, for example, although the Ogaden region is primarily inhabited by pastoral nomads of the Ogaden clan, there is also seasonal movement in and out of the region by Isaq clans to the north, in the centre of what is now the Somaliland Republic. Rain and the grass it produces are the ultimate determinants of movement, other factors (including government intervention) being contingent variables. If rain is evenly distributed in either or both of the two main rainy seasons, spring and autumn, the population will be similarly distributed. If, on the contrary, it falls unevenly, there will be corresponding concentrations of pastoralists. In time of extreme drought, un-precedented nomadic movements in search of grazing take place. Thus in the appalling 1974-75 drought, famine-stricken nomads from the north drove their few surviving camels over 1,000 miles to the hinterland of Mogadishu in search of pasture (for 'normal' patterns of northern nomadic movement see Hunt 1951 and Lewis 1961).

There are two main types of grazing camp, following the division in herding practices associated with sheep and goats (collectively called *adi*) on the one hand and camels on the other. Cattle, if they are owned (as in northwestern and southern Somalia), may form a third herding unit but one whose movements are frequently closely associated with those of sheep and goats, since their watering needs are similar to those of sheep and goats. A married man moves with his wife and young family with sheep and goats, a few milch camels and burden camels to transport the collapsible nomad's tent (*aqal*) from place to place. This domestic unit is known as *guri*, from the verb *gur*, to move. Related families tend to move and camp together, although they also often split up into new combinations. Grazing encampments (sing. *degmo*, from the verb *deg*, to settle) form wherever pasture and water conditions are suitable. Such settlements often consist of 30 or so nuclear or extended families, each camped separately within its own thorn-fence pen, and occupying an area of approximately 20 square miles with a population density of some 20 persons per square mile. Depending on weather conditions, inter-clan relations, government intervention etc., such temporary encampments may only stay in one place for a few weeks and are likely to be separated by large tracts of unoccupied land.

A trend begun in the 1960s in the Togdheer region has been towards more permanent settlement based around cement-lined water tanks (singular, *barkad*) owned by individual families. While water collected at these reservoirs can hardly be withheld from close kin, excess water from the *barkad*s would be sold at great profit in dry areas to which it was transported by truck by enterprising traders. This 'premature settlement', as it has been called, led to much heavier grazing around these new water points, causing widespread erosion, and may have locally exacerbated the effects of the 1974-75 drought.

Following the drought a Central Rangelands Development Project was established, financed by the World Bank, which sought to improve the problem of increasing overgrazing. It combined the balanced provision of water resources with grazing reserves and grazing control. Over the years, mounting population pressure had led to increasingly reckless patterns of livestock over-breeding with short-term survival as the primary goal. There was, moreover, little support among nomads for government efforts to introduce grazing reserves, despite the urgent need for a more rational use of their scarce pastoral resources.

The grazing camel units (the *gel her* as they are called) are in the charge of unmarried men and boys who, from the age of about seven, are sent out to learn the demanding skills of Somali pastoral nomadism. Girls stay with the domestic unit based on sheep and goats, helping their mothers care for these smaller stock and performing other domestic tasks such as grinding grain into flour, cooking, and caring for younger siblings. Men are primarily associated with camels, traditionally the most prized Somali possession and standard of wealth. Men milk camels and cope with the burdensome task of loading and unloading transport camels, though it is women who assemble and dismantle the nomadic tent which is transported on burden camels. The female camels of closely related kin are herded together and congregate in camel camps in an area of suitable pasture. Each camp is a tightly integrated unit. The camel boys, whose diet is chiefly camel's milk augmented occasionally by meat from a slaughtered animal, sleep together at night on a bed of grass in the centre of the kraal. These camel-herdsmen are thus known as 'those who share the same mat' (*arda wadag*). Like the domestic family units with the sheep and goats, a group of camel-camps in an area of grazing has little if any sense of residential solidarity and no fixed composition. However, the tendency of camel-herders of the same lineage to cluster together in an area of pasture is especially pronounced in time of inter-clan hostilities.

These two units—the domestic sheep and goat herding group and the grazing camel unit—are normally most widely separated geographically during the dry seasons when the sheep and goats, which require almost daily watering, have to stay close to the wells while the camels, which can go without water for at least 14 days, will pasture in remote grazing areas. In the summer, especially after the spring *Gu* season's rains, the two stock units, whose water and pasture needs can then be satisfied in close proximity, move closer together. This pattern of dry season dispersal and wet season concentration has important social consequences. In the dry season, preoccupation with the survival of herds and humans is acute. In the wet season there is normally abundant milk, livestock most frequently calve after the rains, and a general expansion of social life takes place. In the dry seasons each family head concentrates on coordinating the watering arrangements of his sheep and goats and his far-flung grazing camels. Pressure on resources is heavy and likely to trigger quarrels over the order of precedence at wells, which quickly develop into violent lineage clashes and the revival of rankling lineage feuds.

The main wet season, in contrast, brings the young herdsmen and marriageable girls together and it is the dating and mating season. It is also the time for other communal rituals, lineage council meetings, and general activity in which there is abundant scope for the oratory and poetising on which Somalis lay such store. This seasonal division between the negative and positive poles of the year is neatly summed up in the proverb 'war and drought; peace and plenty' (*ol iyo abar; nabad iyo 'ano*[1]).

Since rarely more than half a flock is likely to be in milk at the same time, and at the end of the dry season only a much smaller fraction, a family of a wife and a few young children requires a minimum of 50-60 sheep and goats for survival. The minimum camel (or cattle) requirement is similarly 10-15 milch animals. Depending on the family's own labour supply, a flock of 200 or more sheep and goats, say, requires additional help from female relatives. The constant stress on increasing herd size reflects the seasonal uncertainties and the allowance which has to be made for wastage due to drought and disease in this capriciously harsh environment.

Since it is not uncommon for an individual herder to possess over 100 camels worth up to £10,000 (1980s values), it is scarcely realistic to regard all Somali nomads as destitute pastoralists unable to fend for themselves. The problem, however, is that in this uncertain environment a man's riches may disappear almost overnight in the wake of some natural calamity. Thus the Somali nomad is by temperament and practice a gambler who appreciates the transitory nature of success and failure.

---

1   *'ano* means literally milk.

Livestock trade and labour migration

It cannot be emphasised too strongly that pastoral nomadism constitutes the economic base of the vast bulk of the Somali population, and manifestations of the nomadic lifestyle and traditions pervade almost all aspects of Somali life. In contrast to nomadic minorities in other countries, Somalia's nomads are not cut off from the life of urban centres or culturally and socially separated from the majority of urban residents, civil servants and other government employees such as members of the armed forces. From the president downwards, at all levels of government and administration, those living with a modern lifestyle in urban conditions have brothers and cousins living as nomads in the interior and regularly have shares in joint livestock herds. Civil servants commonly invest in livestock, including camels, that are herded by their nomadic kinsmen.

Equally important, the nomads have been for centuries part of a vast, monetised trading network connecting Ethiopia and the Arabian Peninsula. Commercial attitudes are consequently strongly developed. Thus the pastoral nomads have long maintained a distinction between disposable wealth (*mod* in Somali), such as cash; and capital, particularly livestock and above all camels (*mal* in Somali). They have sold livestock and livestock products—hides, skins and clarified butterfat—for centuries. (In contrast, to their neighbours the Afar, who to this day, remain reluctant to sell milk which they consider should not be treated as a commercial commodity.) Sales patterns, however, are influenced by local factors and preferences.

Traditionally, hides and skins are sold in the largest quantities in the dry season, when sheep and goats are slaughtered for food. Camels and cattle, which are traditional stores of wealth (capital assets used in marriage payments, blood money etc.), may not be so readily sold when they are in prime condition in the wet seasons-particularly if cash needs can be satisfactorily met by 'target sales' of less highly valued sheep and goats. Camels, which are the hardiest and most prized wealth, are least readily sold, except by those herdsmen who can afford to do so, or are forced to in order to survive. Hides and skins are sold mainly, but not exclusively, through official channels. Stock on the hoof, on the other hand, are purchased by private merchants for export (mainly) to the Gulf States. The pastoralist seller regularly accompanies the buyer to the port of embarcation, or another main transit centre, and only parts with his stock when he receives a cash payment. Merchants who default on payments to pastoralists are liable to summary imprisonment and may also forfeit their reputation and trade. Brokers (*dilal*) play an important role in this enterprise, using kinship ties as a source of trust and confidence.

It is difficult to generalise about sales patterns since these vary so widely in response to the factors mentioned. However, some indications can be given. From a flock of 100 sheep and goats it would not be unusual to cull 30 head for sale (mainly sheep). From a herd of 100 cattle, 10 might be sold, while from a camel herd of the same size only five might be sold, or killed for consumption.

Northern Somalis have a long tradition of labour migration and overseas employment, which traditionally was mainly crewing on ships. In the decades following independence in 1960, the disparity between local wages in Somalia (higher in the north than the south) and those obtainable in Arabia and the Gulf States led to a large exodus of able-bodied men. This 'muscle-drain' augments the 'brain-drain' to the same countries, and was especially strong in the two decades from the mid-1960s to mid-1980s, and led to a large influx of remittance earnings in cash and kind.

This inflow to dependents and kin, with other factors, led to a marked inflation of prices which were substantially higher in the north than in the south of the country. The ubiquitous transistor radio, so popular among the media-conscious nomads with their powerful oral culture and insatiable appetite for radio, became widely disseminated as part of this influx of goods from kinsmen working overseas. This was only one of the more tangible signs of the extent to which the northern pastoral nomads became part of the modern remittance economy. This developed further and greatly amplified in the 1990s, after Somalia collapsed, with the migration of large numbers of asylum-seekers.

Northern agricultural settlements

In the area of relatively favourable rainfall to the west of Hargeisa in the north, where nomads have turned to cultivation over the last hundred years, there is quite a close association between kinship and land holding. This is the result of the direct settlement of pastoral nomads in this region, where the original 'demonstration effect' was provided by local religious settlements and the adjacent cultivating Oromo (Akishu etc.) of the Jigjiga-Harar area. In this region cultivation, mainly of sorghum and maize, is by ox-drawn plough in much the same style as highland Ethiopian farming. In recent years, new innovations involve the substitution of oxen in ploughing by camels and, on large farms, by tractors.

Villages here, consisting of the houses of related families grouped together within a common thorn fence, may contain as many as 20 nuclear families with small stock (sheep and goats) and cattle penned at night within the village fence. The majority of these farmers own, or are part owners of herds of camels and flocks of sheep and goats tended by close kin in the best available pastures, often many miles from these farming settlements. Typically, a man with several wives will station one in a farming settlement with her children and flocks, while another is sent out with flocks of sheep and goats and some milch camels to distant pastures.

Most of these farming settlements expand in population at harvest time or in the dry autumn months when sheep and goats return from the southern pastures in the Haud and Ogaden, and camels move closer to the dry-season home wells. Village settlements are based on artificial ponds (singular, *war*) excavated and maintained collectively by the users who also regularly collaborate in harvesting. Each nuclear family has a plot of land of between a quarter acre and one acre in extent, of which usually only part is planted each year. Grass on the fallow land provides pasture for young stock and the stubble left after the harvest affords useful grazing for cattle in the dry winter months. Yields vary with the size of holding, between 4 and 12 x 200 lb bags. Excess grain is stored in pit granaries dug in the centre of settlements.

Southern agricultural settlements

Unlike their northern counterparts, the Digil and Rahanweyn (and some Hawiye) who practise mixed farming along the banks and between the Juba and Shebelle rivers in southern Somalia have a history of cultivation going back several centuries. The plough is not used traditionally in tilling the ground, this work being done instead by hand-hoe (*yambo*) in a system of cultivation which, according to some authorities, is particularly well adapted to the inter-riverine soils with their outstanding natural tilth. The chief crop in the dry-farming region of Bay is *durra* (sorghum, *misego* in Somali), whereas in the higher rainfall areas of middle and lower Shebelle the main crop is maize (*gelay*). Subsidiary crops are sesame (*simsim*), beans *(digir)*, squashes (*bu'ur*), bananas (*mus*), cotton (*suf*), sugar cane *(kassab)*, and groundnuts (*buri*). Sesame is often planted after the spring *gu* rains, and maize after the autumn *dayr* rains; usually sorghum is first planted after the *gu* and a second crop is grown in the *dayr*. Both grains are stored in pit granaries where, although losing some of its value as seed, sorghum can keep for over ten years and still be suitable for domestic consumption.

Most of the bananas which are so important for export, and the sugar used for internal consumption, are grown on estates, many of them privately owned, along the Shebelle and Juba rivers. The

59

oldest established riverine cultivators are people of mixed Somali and Swahili origin, some descended from former slaves imported from East Africa to serve as agricultural serfs for pastoral Somali landlords. Known as 'tough-haired' (*tima-adag*) and traditionally despised by the nomads, these people still provide the bulk of the unskilled labour force in the riverine plantation industry, and live in villages under headmen. They suffered terribly at the hands of the pastoralist Somali militias in the conflicts of the early 1990s in southern Somalia.

In the dry farming upland Bay area, away from the rivers, a village settlement (*bullo, bildan* or *billed*) is based around ponds (singular, *war*) owned by the man or men who organised the original work of excavation. There is a well-established code of water management designed to safeguard the water and prevent its pollution by clothes washing, human defecation etc. Water-guards are organised at night, especially when water is scarce, and access granted only to members of the community. Similar cooperative parties provide the individual farmer with help in the heavy work of cultivation, clearing virgin bush, planting and harvesting, and also in building the characteristic local mud and wattle hut (*mundille*). Villages range in size from settlements of 20 to over a hundred houses, and include nuclear or extended families. Village populations thus range from approximately 100 to 1,000 men, women and children. The larger villages depend on several ponds and contain Quranic schools, mosques and other local facilities. Each married man, with about three dependents, normally has cultivating rights in at least one field. About two hectares of sorghum are planted in the spring rain season, some-times intercropped with cowpeas. The corresponding yield in an average year is about 2,000 kg. As in tending small stock, women play an important role in cultivation—in planting, weeding and harvesting.

The technique of cultivation is very distinctive. The field to be planted is first cleared of weeds and stubble from the previous season's crop. Once this has been done the field is divided into neat squares called *mos*, approximately 2m x 2m. Each side is two paces long. A strip of 40 or 50 squares constitutes the land measure known as a 'staff' *('ul)*. A series of twelve such strips constitutes a plot known as a *darab* measuring approximately a quarter of a hectare. The squares have ridges to catch and retain rainwater, so that the plot looks like a contoured or relief chessboard. The ridges are traditionally built with the aid of a heavy blunt wooden rake called *kewawa*. It is worked by a team of two men. One pushes with the handle while the other pulls from the opposite side with the attached rope. The man who is pushing the *kewawa* stands on the inside of the *moos*, shaping the loose top soil into a ridge while his companion stands outside, pulling the rope. The first man then turns at an angle of 45 degrees, the other steps or jumps over to face him and they start on the next side. When that ridge is shaped the second man turns to face in his original direction while the first moves to face him. This diagonal dance is carried on across the field, producing a step pattern of ridges. As this is crossed repeatedly it forms squares which eventually fill the field.

This is heavy work. It takes two men a full day to till a *darab* of land in this way. Sowing is another day's work. At least four days' work will be required for weeding, and one to three to harvest the crop. If, as is common when the rains are reasonable, both a spring and an autumn crop are planted, the total minimum labour input required is thus of the order of 20 man days per *darab*. If two hectares (i.e. 8 *darab*s) are planted the minimum labour requirement is thus of the order of 160 man-days. This, of course, makes no allowance for intercropping, ancillary weeding, driving off birds which attack the grain as it ripens, and storage of the product in pit granaries, or its sale in market stores.

Despite the age of village settlements in this region and the heterogeneous character of the local Digil and Rahanweyn population with its layer upon layer of adopted clients, villages do not traditionally have headmen like those found among the riverine population. Political allegiance, like land-rights, is ultimately vested in lineages; identification with a lineage extends outside villages to the clan as both a territorial and a kin group. Clan elders interact with governmental authority in a particular area. Village solidarity, involving among other facilities the labour of the young men under a local leader, presents a potential for further local political organisation.

The majority of the Digil and Rahanweyn farmers also keep livestock, each family possessing, according to a 1977 FAO/ World Bank report, on average 10 animal units (five camels, three cattle and four sheep and goats). Where, as is common, extended families have more livestock the head of the family (the father or the eldest of a group of brothers) stays at home on the farm, while younger kinsmen move semi-nomadically with cattle and other animals.

True nomads (some of whom belong to the Digil and Rahanweyn confederacies) also move through the inter-riverine region seasonally, often with large herds of camels. The most commonly seen are groups belonging to the Galje'el (the name means 'camel-lovers') and Garre clans; the former are usually classified as Hawiye, the latter as Digil. The young camel-herders of these groups are known for their distinctive Afro-style hair-do called in Somali *gud*. Their herding settlements are organised in the same way as those described above for the northern nomads. As might be expected, these people have much wider ranging movements and connections than the more sedentary Digil and Rahanweyn. The latter are additionally isolated by their distinctive speech (Afmaymay) which is not readily understood by other Somalis.

State settlement schemes following the 'Drought of the Long Tail'

Almost a quarter of a million nomads, mainly from the northeastern region of the Republic, lost most of their livestock in the devastating drought of 1974-75. A large number of these destitute pastoralists were resettled in state farms and fishing settlements, chiefly in the south. The largest agricultural settlements, with populations of approximately 20-30,000, were in the Lower Shebelle and Middle Juba regions, with intensive cultivation based on irrigation and a considerable degree of mechanisation. These huge enterprises (among which the main schemes were Kurtunwarre, Sablale and Dujuma) produced a mixture of crops including sorghum and rice, and had an elaborate and rather artificial social organisation purportedly designed to encourage the process of detribalisation and the growth of patriotism. The organisation, in groups of family communities, was rather theoretical, while in actual practice there was more direction by officials of the relevant ministries which provided the necessary technical expertise. Families received rations, medical care, schooling and other social services and a small wage in return for their labour. Fishing settlements were established at Brava and elsewhere along the coast. These enterprises in which there was a more immediate return in the shape of regular fish catches were run as cooperatives, and the most successful appeared to be the smallest.

There are traditional precedents for the transformation of Somali pastoral nomads into cultivators—not only those in Galbed Region, but also the Digil and Rahanweyn who derive in part from northern nomads who settled in the inter-river region over many centuries. There have also always been fishing communities on the Somali coasts, such as the 'Rer Manjo', on the margins of the dominant nomadic culture. Although both those occupations are despised by the proud nomads, they have clearly been adopted from time to time by pastoral drop-outs with no other hope of survival.

There was thus some precedent for the vast drought-relief settlement programme. The results, however, tended to illustrate the resilience of the pastoral culture. The agricultural settlements, especially, lost a substantial proportion of the men who originally settled in them as destitute nomads. As their home grazing areas improved in the cycle of good seasons that so often follows a succession of drought years, men drifted back to resume herding, leaving women and children behind in the settlements where they received food, health care and education. Some nomads saved enough from settlement wages, rations and other sources to send money to distant relatives, instructing them to invest in livestock on their behalf. In due course, when the makings of a new herd had been put together, men left the settlement covertly and moved back to their familiar pastures where sheep and goats reproduce quickly under optimal conditions. Others joined the 'muscle-drain' of migrant workers in the Gulf States, an option which was eventually made less easy as the Somali government imposed tighter passport control. A similar, though less drastic exodus of men occurred from the fishing settlements where there was at least a protein catch to substitute for livestock, and where conditions, especially in the smaller cooperatives, were less regimented.

The refugee crisis (1978–80)

The vast exodus of ethnic Somalis and Oromos and other peoples from Western Somalia/Eastern Ethiopia, in the wake of the 1977/78 Ogaden war, imposed an even more crippling burden on Somalia than the natural disaster of 1974. As the guerrilla war waged by the Western Somali Liberation Front and their allies the Abo and Oromo Liberation Fronts continued, the influx of refugees from Ethiopia became overwhelming. From some 400,000 refugees registered in camps in December 1979, a year later the figure had more than doubled, with a corresponding increase in the number of camps to over 30. Outside the camps, as many as another half million were estimated to have found hospitality as 'invisible refugees' living with relatives, further straining the fragile economy of the country with its acute foreign exchange problems. By the end of 1980 virtually one out of every four people in Somalia was a refugee; the fact that the majority of refugees were ethnic Somalis with kinsmen in the Republic blurred the otherwise appalling impact of this statistic. The paradox was that these pathetically uprooted war victims were refugees in a state based on their own ethnic identity: they were, as it were, refugees 'at home'. But their real home, to which they sought to return, was the Ogaden and, in the case of Oromo refugees, Sidamo and Bale provinces of Ethiopia.

Transit reception camps were set up at key points on the border with Ethiopia, and the main camps, containing up to 50,000 people each, were further inside Somalia. The character of the camps' population partly reflected what might be called the political demography of the refugees' situation. Numerous surveys by the UN and other agencies in the camps found that the majority of refugees were women, young children and old men. Most of the menfolk who had camels still surviving in the Ogaden stayed there with their herds. This applied particularly to the young men, the traditional camel-boys and warriors, who remained behind with these livestock and lent their support to the Western Somali Liberation Front guerrillas.

Thus the demographic make-up of the camp population reflected the traditional division of labour and herding units in the nomadic economy. Other refugees outside the camps did in some cases bring their livestock, especially small stock (sheep and goats) with them. The presence of this additional animal population, while providing food, also increased the erosion of scarce grazing in the Republic, and the wood and charcoal cooking-fuel needs of all the refugees led to further serious pressure on the country's limited forest and scrub bush resources. Indeed, by the end of 1980, it was proving necessary to import fuel for domestic cooking in the camps.

While external humanitarian and governmental agencies played a crucial role in trying to feed and clothe the refugees as well as providing medical supplies, Somalia at an early stage responded to this crisis in an exemplary fashion. Relief work was organised by the Somali Refugee Commission, directed by the minister of Local Government and Rural Development. Over 2,000 Somali personnel from most of the country's ministries were involved in this task on which the Somali government had by July 1980 spent over £16 million from its own slender resources. The humanitarian needs of the refugees received initially little publicity, despite Somali efforts, and it took many months for the international community to register the magnitude of the calamity and respond appropriately.

As far as the internal organisation of the main refugee camps was concerned, they were divided into sections or quarters, which were usually named by the refugees after places in the Ogaden from which they came. At the same time, efforts were made by the government to introduce the same scheme of decimal divisions and subdivisions of communities (overriding traditional clan divisions) that had been imposed in the agricultural and fishing settlements established for the victims of the 1974 drought.

Although some efforts, with varying degrees of success, were made to promote cultivation, poultry-keeping and crafts in some of the camps, none was anywhere near being self-sufficient. The stark fact remained that the economy of the country simply did not possess the resources to absorb so many uprooted people, even when the majority were ethnically Somali and indeed kinsmen. This major economic aspect of the refugee situation was reinforced by the political aspiration—on the part of the refugees themselves as much as the government—to return to the country from which they had been forced to flee by what they saw as Ethiopian imperialism. After all, the Ogaden region takes its name from the Somali people who traditionally inhabit it and whose aspirations for self-determination did not necessarily mean an unqualified desire to merge with the Republic. Aid for the refugees became an important source of general national aid and long-term responsibility for this new aid industry was borne by the Office of the UN High Commissioner for Refugees (UNHCR), financed by member governments at an annual cost of $100 million. The National Refugee Commission, a branch of the Interior Ministry, was run by two Refugee Commissioners; one, known officially as the Extraordinary Commissioner, was a senior Ogadeni general. The actual number of refugees (which directly affected the aid budget) was highly controversial, the Somali authorities resisting all UNHCR attempts to enumerate them but settling for a 'planning figure' of 700,000. The male population of the camps provided a captive reserve source of manpower for illegal recruitment into Somalia's armed forces.

Internal dissent after the Ogaden war

At its height, the Ogaden war was immensely popular in Somalia and President Siyad's public standing never higher. The terrible defeat and the refugee influx (which seriously upset the existing clan demography) quickly led to widespread public demoralisation and to an upsurge of 'tribalism' (i.e. clan loyalties) as different groups sought scapegoats to explain the debacle. Thus, hard on the heels of the Somali retreat, an unsuccessful attempted coup was mounted against the regime in April 1978. This was led by military officers of the Mijerteyn (Darod) clan who had played a dominant role in the old civilian governments. After the failure of this attempted coup, those who had escaped arrest regrouped, forming a guerrilla opposition group called the Somali Salvation Democratic Front (SSDF) which made its operational headquarters across the border in Ethiopia. After some initial successes— with Ethiopian support—this organisation and its clan base in Somalia were savagely subdued. That the Mijerteyn sought support in Ethiopia, Somalia's traditional enemy, is both a sign of their desperation and a measure of the degree of disintegration of Somali national (and clan-family, e.g. Darod) solidarity. All the measures of Siyad's Scientific Socialism had evidently not, after all, succeeded in their task of transforming Somali national solidarity from the ancient 'organic' to the modern 'mechanical' mode (to borrow the terminology of the famous French Sociologist, Emile Durkheim).

In 1989-90 the spotlight fell on the main protagonist in the recent civil war in Somalia, the Somali National Movement (SNM) which, despite its name, drew most of its support from the Isaq clans of central northern Somalia and articulated their profound disaffection from the Siyad regime. Following the example of the SSDF, the SNM was able to make its operational headquarters across the border in Ethiopia from which it launched a number of daring raids. From the early 1980s, the north was administered by increasingly harsh military rule emanating from the capital, with savage reprisals meted out to the local population, who were assumed to be pro-SNM and subjected to severe economic as well as political harassment. The north, as could clearly be seen in 1985, to a foreign observer began to look and feel like a downtrodden colony under alien military tyranny. Indeed, this was how it was perceived locally.

Armed opposition to Siyad was spreading and assuming a national character transcending clan divisions. But, at the same time, despite their common objective—the overthrow of Siyad Barre—the predominantly Darod and Isaq bases, respectively, of the SSDF and SNM added to their other logistical difficulties, preventing them from making common cause, and so weakened the overall impact of their rebellion.

Since the Ogaden war defeat, Siyad had still continued to support, albeit somewhat nominally, the Ogadeni Western Somali Liberation Front which remained an irksome thorn in Ethiopia's side. However, the destabilising pressures exerted by the SSDF and SNM had the effect of driving President Siyad to seek an accommodation with Ethiopia, a move that was also encouraged by Somalia's Western allies (Italy, the EC and the USA). The Somali regime's anxiety to secure a deal with Ethiopia was increased by the insecurity that his clansmen felt when the President had a nearly fatal car crash in May 1986. Siyad, nevertheless, proved remarkably resilient, and at the end of that year, having recovered from the accident, he was re-elected unopposed (since no opposition was permitted) as head of state for a further seven-year term.

A 'new' government was formed in February 1987. For the first time since the coup, however, the cabinet now included a 'Prime Minister' in the curious shape of the faithful General Samater (Siyad's long-serving and politically unassuming military commander). In reality, however, President Siyad had consolidated the position of his own clan and family, within which rivalry was beginning to surface over who should eventually succeed him. The Marrehan now unquestionably and openly dominated the military, and Siyad's son, General Masleh, was put in charge of a special northern command unit. The old MOD (Marrehan, Ogaden, Dulbahante) Darod alliance was beginning to crumble, at least at the highest levels, as the Marrehan closed ranks in the face of mounting insecurity. The time had come to secure Ethiopia's cooperation in cauterising the SNM and SSDF.

3

THE COLLAPSE IN
SOUTHERN SOMALIA

Peace with Ethiopia, chaos at home

Further signalling the demise of pan-Somali solidarity, in April 1988 President Siyad and Ethiopia's Mengistu Haile Mariam finally signed a peace accord, normalising their relations and undertaking to stop supporting each other's dissidents. Thus Siyad withdrew support from the WSLF (which was by now opposed by an anti-Siyad organisation, the Ogaden National Liberation Front). Mengistu, for his part, withdrew support from the SSDF (to which he had previously assigned Ethiopian equipment and troops), and similarly stopped backing the SNM. Knowledge of this détente, and fear of its consequences, triggered the SNM's audacious onslaught on military installations in Northern Somalia, which quickly led to the all-out civil war in 1988-91 between the regime and Somaliland's Isaq clansmen.

The human cost was terrible. Thousands of civilians were killed and wounded, and at least half a million fled their homes seeking asylum across the border in Ethiopia and in the Republic of Djibouti. Thousands of refugees eventually found refuge in Canada, Britain, Scandinavia, Italy and the USA. Meanwhile, male Ogadeni refugees in northern Somalia, who had long been subject to illegal conscription into Siyad's armed forces, were forced to join a paramilitary militia to fight the SNM and to man checkpoints on the roads. Ogadeni refugees were encouraged to take over the remains of Isaqi shops and houses in what, after bombardment by Siyad's forces, were effectively ghost towns. Thus those who had been earlier received as refugee guests in northern Somalia had supplanted their Isaqi hosts, and many of the latter, in this bitterly ironic turn of fate, had become refugees in the Ogaden.

If the Ogadenis were once the tail that wagged the dog, drawing Somalia into their fight for liberation from Ethiopian rule, the situation in 1989-90 was very different. Those still in the Ogaden were to all intents and purposes deserted by Siyad, while those inside Somalia were co-opted into fighting to maintain the regime. Here the appeal, also addressed to the disunited Mijerteyn, was for Darod solidarity against the Isaq. Thus other northern Darod clans were armed by the regime and urged to join the fight. Other northern groups (such as the Esa and the Gadabursi) who are neither Isaq nor Darod were also armed and exhorted to turn against the Isaq. The regime's appeal for Darod solidarity evoked a corresponding attempt by the Isaq to invoke a wider-based, higher-level 'Irrir' solidarity to include the important Hawiye clans in whose territory Mogadishu is located. While seeking Darod support where appropriate, the regime also endeavoured to secure the loyalty of all non-Isaq clans and, of course, to penetrate the ranks of the Isaq. Thus, in its desperate fight for survival, Siyad's family and clansmen sought to exploit to the full segmentary lineage rivalry within the Somali nation. They also made abundant use of coercion and rewards of all kinds, as corruption flourished.

By the end of January 1991, the SNM had effectively overcome Siyad's forces in the north and was consolidating its position throughout the region. Many Ogadeni refugees had returned to their homes in Ethiopia which were now incorporated in three 'autonomous' regions within the Ethiopian state. Mutinous

Ogadeni soldiery in southern Somalia had established in 1989 the Somali Patriotic Movement which joined the loose coalition of movements fighting Siyad, especially the recently formed United Somali Congress.

Partly derived from an earlier association with the SNM, the USC had become primarily a Hawiye organisation with two main factions, one based on the Abgal clan, whose home town was Mogadishu, and the other based on the Habar Gidir, the clan of the USC militia commander General Aideed (himself a former general in Siyad's army and former ambassador to India). Siyad naturally sought to exploit these divisions as well as exhorting all the Darod in Mogadishu to kill the Hawiye citizens whether they were Abgal or Habar Gidir. The ensuing interclan violence, however, threatened Siyad's position further, and in desperation he finally turned his heavy artillery on the Hawiye quarters of the city. This provoked the general uprising, an extremely bloody one, which led to Siyad's flight from the city on 26 January 1991, pursued, not far behind, by General Aideed who had recently entered Mogadishu with his forces.

While Aideed was thus engaged in chasing Siyad, the USC Abgal group in Mogadishu hastily set up an 'interim government' under Ali Mahdi (a prominent Abgal businessman and warlord) as 'provisional president', with ministers drawn from members of other non-Hawiye clans—not all of whom had accepted their appointments or even been consulted about them! When this largely self-appointed administration began to try to control the numerous armed groups at large in Mogadishu, the Habar Gidir became suspicious of Abgal intentions, and fighting erupted between the two Hawiye clans. With the calling of a USC party congress in July 1991, at which Aideed was elected USC Chairman with Ali Mahdi continuing as 'interim president', an uneasy peace was restored.

Meanwhile, Siyad and his remaining henchmen had fled to his clan territory in Gedo where he proceeded to attempt to mobilise and manipulate wider level pan-Darod solidarity, forming the

Marrehan-based Somali National Front. Appeals to Darod unity were encouraged by the indiscriminate revenge killing of people of this clan-family (especially those of the Dulbahante clan associated with the NSS) perpetrated by Hawiye groups in the aftermath of Siyad's escape from Mogadishu. Thus a motley array of Darod-based forces (including for a time some SPM and SSDF, as well as Marrehan) became engaged in a series of skirmishes in the area between Mogadishu and the port of Kismayu to the south, and Afgoi and Baidoa to the west and north. In April 1991, after heavy fighting and at the cost of a renewed exodus to Ethiopia and Kenya of thousands of Darod refugees, the USC gained control of Kismayu—losing it again later in the year, but recovering it in the spring of 1992.

The rebirth of Somaliland

During the long period of confused clan manoeuvring and turmoil in the south, the USC 'interim government' in Mogadishu sent its Isaq Prime Minister (a Somalilander) and other ministers on largely fruitless missions abroad to seek international aid and recognition. Appreciating that external recognition would require widespread internal support, Ali Mahdi's government tried at the same time to persuade the SNM and other movements to join in talks aimed at the formation of an acceptable national government. Most publicly this was pursued at the abortive Djibouti conferences of July 1991. That the USC Prime Minister, Omar Arteh, was a well-known Isaq figure might have been expected to facilitate these complex negotiations. Actually it had the reverse effect. He had been appointed without consultation with the SNM who, in any case, regarded him as tainted by too close association with Siyad, as well as possessing other undesirable features. Hence the SNM, whose links with the USC were in any case through Aideed and the Habar Gidir rather than Ali Mahdi, responded coolly to these overtures. This cautious response seemed amply justified as the magnitude of internal USC divisions became plain in the developing conflict and chaos in and around Mogadishu.

Therefore the SNM concentrated on its own local problems in the north. A surprising degree of peace between the Isaq and non-Isaq clans of the region had been secured, largely through the efforts of the traditional clan elders, by the time of the SNM national congress in May 1991. There was widespread hatred and distrust of the south (identified with Siyad's misrule) and a strong tide of public feeling favouring separatism. Bowing to this, the SNM leadership proclaimed on 18 May 1991 that their region would resume its independence from the south, taking the title 'Somaliland Republic'. This pragmatic decision reflected the desire of many of the people of Somaliland to get on with rebuilding their devastated country and ruined towns, after their destruction by Siyad's forces which had left hundreds of thousands of land-mines to remind northerners of that barbaric regime.

Somalia had thus now reverted to its two former constituent colonial units, the ex-British and ex-Italian Somalilands—a development that was bitterly, but ineffectually opposed by Ali Mahdi's nominal administration in Mogadishu. There were now two interim governments, neither of which recognised the other, and each of which desperately sought international emergency aid and diplomatic recognition. While the SNM government had initially virtually country-wide support, Ali Mahdi's government was effectively restricted to the Mogadishu area, and after September 1991 only to a dwindling part of the city itself. Outside Mogadishu, a plethora of locally based clan militias reigned and struggled for control of wider areas.

The same tendencies of reversion to clan loyalties, with alliance and dissociation of segmentary kin groups according to the local context, characterised the general scene throughout the Somali region in 1992. Siyad's much-publicised official campaigns against clan allegiance had obviously had no positive lasting effect, which was not surprising since they were essentially rhetorical. Indeed,

Siyad's own power politics always included a powerful clan-based element and served to reinforce and exacerbate ancient antagonisms in the segmentary lineage system—which, of course, he did not invent. He well knew how to adapt the ancient divide-and-rule formula to these particular clan conditions. He befriended groups which enabled him to attack his clan enemies. In this pattern of what has been aptly called 'clan clientelism', Siyad distributed arms and money to his friends, encouraging them to attack his enemies who, naturally, were accused of divisive 'tribalism' by the master tribalist.

The legacy of Siyad's rule, including making peace with Ethiopia (thus removing this factor of external threat), contributed materially to the ensuing post-Siyad period in which the Somali nation became more deeply divided along its traditional kinship lines than perhaps at any other time in the twentieth century. Here we might suggest that, if the segmentary system had not already existed, Siyad would have invented it as a mechanism to cling to power at the vortex of clan chaos. By destroying his country's economy through corruption and inefficiency, Siyad also promoted those conditions of scarce resources and insecurity on which clan loyalty thrives, since clan solidarity then offers the only hope of survival. And by providing arms—directly and indirectly—Siyad's legacy of Marrehan misrule ensured a wide and persistent prevalence of extremely bloody clan conflict.

The pan-Somali ideal, founded in cultural identity rather than political unity evoked in opposition to the colonial situation, after being so strong in the 1950s and 1960s had taken a severe battering. In 1991/92, reactively influenced by the examples of the SNM, SSDF, USC and SPM, the general tendency was for every major Somali clan to form its own militia movement. Thus clans became effectively self-governing entities throughout the Somali region as they carved out spheres of influence in a process which, with the abundance of modern weapons, frequently entailed bitter conflicts with a high toll of civilian casualties.

Hence the political geography of the Somali hinterland in 1992 closely resembled that reported by European explorers in the nineteenth century, with spears replaced by Kalashnikovs and bazookas. These clan domains could only be entered or traversed by outsiders—people of other clans and foreigners—with the consent of the locals and usually the payment of appropriate fees for 'protection'. This was the situation confronting those intrepid non-governmental agencies which still operated in this extremely dangerous region.

Clan politics, however, has never been characterised by hard and fast alliances limited to the clan level. Related clans can and do ally in wider formations as circumstances dictate, and by the same token fall apart. So, as we have seen, the USC faction leaders in Mogadishu, however divided among themselves internally, are perceived externally as being all Hawiye. This tends to trigger a corresponding reactive alliance of the various Darod clan fractions at a higher level of Darod unity, and similarly among the Isaq clans of the north. By the same token, the tensions and conflicts which broke out among the Isaq in the Somaliland Republic's first years of existence were linked to the fact that once the Isaq had made peace with their non-Isaq neighbours (the Gadabursi, Isa, Dulbahante and Warsangeli) they were more likely to be divided internally. Their ultimately largely successful resolution of conflict by panels of local clan elders is a truly remarkable achievement. As we shall see later, this process—crucially, a homemade one, slowly unfolding from grass roots moots—proved incomparably more effective than the high profile top-down 'peace process' that has failed so miserably in southern Somalia.

International intervention in Somalia

Outside Somaliland, and further south, order only existed in the SSDF-controlled northeastern region, largely thanks to the close relationship between this Front and the local Mijerteyn clan elders.

Elsewhere, as we have seen, Somalia was divided into a dozen or more clan-based polities controlled by clan elders and local warlords. The resulting chaos, combined with the continuing drought, resulted in a devastating famine in which half a million people were estimated to have perished. International relief aid was routinely looted and stolen from the starving. Under media pressure and other humanitarian pressure, in April 1992 the UN Security Council authorised the first of a series of peace-keeping and famine relief operations to Somalia. The first, the United Nations Operation in Somalia (UNOSOM), was a relatively small operation, designed to monitor and help sustain the ceasefire between the warring factions that had been negotiated by the UN in March 1992. However, as this proved to lack the necessary persuasive power a new American-led force known as UNITAF, with 37,000 personnel (26,000 of them American), was launched in December 1992 under the optimistic title 'Operation Restore Hope'.

In fact, in the initial calm that greeted this unprecedented intrusion it took the heavily armed and well-equipped UN force only a few weeks to secure Somalia's main ports and roads to enable relief supplies to flow freely. But Somalis with weapons were soon in evidence on the streets again as security deteriorated. This prompted aggressive patrolling, disarming those carrying weapons, and raiding the notorious arms market in Mogadishu. More daringly, direct attacks were launched against militia forces of the two notorious warlords, Aideed and Morgan (Mohamed Siyad Hersi, who had risen to prominence in the Siyad era, prudently marrying one of the 'Old Man's' daughters).

In an apparent lull in the inter-clan conflict in southern Somalia, a ceasefire agreement was signed on 27 March 1993 by the leading warlords and others which, *inter alia*, committed the parties to 'complete disarmament' and empowered UN forces to take strong action against defaulters. At the same time it was agreed at the UN that the US UNITAF force, which was due to withdraw, would be replaced by UNOSOM II, with personnel drawn from a large number of countries and under the command of a Turkish General with a US deputy. This new force took over at the beginning of May, by which time none of the provisions of the March agreement had been implemented and new supplies of weapons were reaching the warlords. On 5 June a Pakistani contingent was ambushed as it was about to inspect some of Aideed's arms stores, close to his radio station. Twenty-four Pakistani blue berets were killed and others wounded. The UN treated this as an outrage, helicopter gunship strikes were authorised on Aideed's bases in Mogadishu and he himself was branded as an 'outlaw' with a generous price on his head. Typically, he responded by placing the same price on the head of UNOSOM's leader. There was now all-out war in Mogadishu between Aideed's clansmen and other supporters and UNOSOM. At the beginning of October 1993, in the bloody incident which became known as 'Black Hawk down', Aideed's forces succeeded in shooting down helicopter gunships as they strafed the streets of Mogadishu. US television news broadcast grisly pictures of dead US personnel being dragged through the streets of Mogadishu, prompting a public furore. Clearly UNOSOM II was doomed. Clinton, who had been elected in 1992, was forced to announce that all US forces would quit Somalia by 31 March 1994. For all their sophisticated technology, the Americans had been repeatedly outsmarted by local Somalis. They had committed incredible blunders, such as hiring local transport and administrative personnel from members of Aideed's clan who were extremely efficient in passing on intelligence to their kinsmen.

The US President's announcement quickly led to the other national components of UNOSOM leaving as soon as they could. Hectic UN action then followed to try to restore the defunct peace agreement between Aideed, Ali Mahdi and other warlords so that something positive could appear to have been achieved by this fiasco. As usual, the negotiators agreed to cease hostilities, and further to prepare for a national reconciliation conference in

May which would result in the formation of an interim government. There was, however, as usual no progress in political reconstruction, and UNOSOM's mandate was reduced from peace enforcement to peace keeping. Most of the Western contingents had now gone, being replaced by Third World troops who were left to prepare for the last stage of the operation and its disbandment in March 1995.

The final exodus was marked in Mogadishu by extensive looting as the UN base, built with Somalia's aid budget, was besieged by Somali scavengers. A few months later, as the country again began to descend into chaos, the very foundations of the $160-million UN headquarters had disappeared. With money from the sale of this scrap and other discarded equipment, a new generation of faction leaders and warlords was rising to prominence. One of these Hawiye entrepreneurs was the stone merchant Muuse Soodi Yalahow, based in Jowhar on the northern edge of Mogadishu, who was destined to replace Ali Mahdi as a leading Abgal warlord. Another rising star was the Habar Gidir financier Osman Ali Atto, who belonged to the Sa'ad lineage like Aideed and had served as his finance adviser. He had successfully developed a number of large garage workshops for constructing heavily armed 'technicals', imported pick ups (jeeps or other) , adapted for combat by the addition(usually) of a machine gun at the front and a light artillery piece, or even anti-aircraft gun on the back. (These modern vehicles were a development of the armed Ford pick up trucks, used so successfully by the British 'Desert Rats' against Rommel in North Africa in 1942.) By 2002, this self-made entrepreneur, whose father had been a camel-herder, controlled half the small airport of Jezira and a strategic checkpoint at the southern entrance to Mogadishu.

After conflict between the Habar Gidir and Abgal over their rival banana export interests in April 1996, Aideed himself was killed in a skirmish in Mogadishu in August. His son Hussein Aideed (a former US marine who had served in Operation Restore Hope as an interpreter) attempted to assume the mantle of his father and made a bid to form a government. Hopes that he might be a voice for peace were soon dispelled as he boycotted the latest 'peace talks' in Ethiopia, and at the end of November he and his clansmen were engaged in some of the fiercest fighting of the year. The future appeared bleak.

The Arta transitional government

However at the beginning of 2000 the new President of Djibouti, Ismail Omar Geele, launched a new and novel peace plan for Somalia under the auspices of the local regional organisation IGAD (the Intergovernmental Authority on Development, comprising Somalia, Djibouti, Eritrea, Kenya, Sudan, Ethiopia and Uganda). The EU, UN and US, as well as Egypt, Italy and Libya, quickly endorsed the project which was to mount a Somali conference in Djibouti, at the hillside resort of Arta. Unlike previous efforts, this was billed as a grassroots endeavour (with some similarity to the successful peace conferences in Somaliland), with 'delegates' and 'representatives' across the clan spectrum and embracing all the social categories of what was optimistically called 'civil society'—traditional elders, religious scholars, 'intellectuals' (i.e. persons with some higher education), artists (chiefly poets and singers), and women (*sic*). With UN assistance, it was claimed, this wide array of people could assume responsibility as protagonists 'in the peace process' (a concept as questionable as that of 'civil society', however familiar in Development jargon).

Although they could not be excluded entirely, the warlords who had such a deplorable record in this field were not ideal delegates. A serious problem never properly addressed was, of course, how to test the representative character of 'delegates'. In practice many people who claimed to be duly appointed representatives were simply self-appointed, and this remained one of

81

the most obvious flaws in the whole process which nevertheless sought to include people drawn from every section of the nation in the widest sense, with representatives of minorities as well as of major groups. The former US Ambassador and head of UNOSOM I, Robert Oakley, dropping in on the conference, looked around the familiar faces gathered there and jokingly asked, 'Where is Siyad?'; in fact about 60 per cent of the 245 members of the assembly were estimated to be former members of Siyad's carefully selected parliament.

For the first time openly reflecting political realities, membership of the resulting assembly was based on clan quotas (and more curiously gender), and seats were allocated accordingly: 44 seats each for Darod, Hawiye, Digil Mirifle, and Dir clan-families (this was controversial since Somaliland, which boycotted the meeting, contained a significant number of Dir); 24 for 'minorities', 25 for women, and the balance of 20 picked randomly by the Djibouti President (for no very good reason). In the event, the assembly chose as President of the resulting national assembly and 'Transitional National Government' (TNG) Abdiqasim Salad Hassan (nicknamed 'Salad Boy' for his light-hearted manner), a former enthusiastic exponent of Siyad's Scientific Socialism and at one point minister of the Interior. As a Habar Gidir, who had now developed an Islamist orientation and who espoused Hawiye unity, he was deemed well suited to lead his fractious clansmen in Mogadishu. But when they moved to Mogadishu, things turned out rather differently. Despite ardent support from UN officials, whose grasp of Somali realities was always weak, and from some Arab countries—and of course Italy—the TNG proved singularly unpopular and never succeeded in controlling more than a few streets in the capital. Two years after Arta it collapsed, retaining only a fantasy existence promoted by the UN and the Italians, with the unhelpful result of concealing and confusing the real situation in southern Somalia.

The Mbagathi Transitional Federal Government

The next external international attempt to restore Somalia opened in Kenya, at Mbagathi, in October 2002, supported again by IGAD with strong involvement of the EC and UN who covered most of the costs. Ethiopia and Kenya, which had experienced Somali irredentism in the past, were both strongly involved. Although these talks were attended by fewer people, a special point this time was the inclusion of all the main warlords which the organizers evidently considered would give greater weight to the deliberations of the participants, and to the status of the government that it was hoped would result from it. This hope, never clearly articulated publicly, paid little attention to the past record of warlords as having shown no sense of patriotism or civic responsibility in their wanton attacks on people and property. Those, for example, exercising control over coastal areas had happily sold to foreign interests fishing rights as well as rights to dump waste—often toxic. Their indiscriminate lust for pecuniary gain was perhaps best illustrated by their readiness to act as undercover US agents in the search for Somali 'Islamic extremists'.

With an unprecedented amount of foreign intervention (especially from EU officials), more rampant corruption, massive vote buying, and more fraudulent claims for the representative capacity of many candidates than had occurred in any previous Somali electoral process, a new 'transitional assembly' for Somalia, with a similar mixed clan proportion of members, was eventually cobbled together. Many of the so-called 'delegates' could not safely return to their declared places of origin! It was thus entirely in character that this fractious body, notable for the colourful fist-fights involved in its later stages, took two years to reach a conclusion, eventually choosing as provisional president the Ethiopian candidate, Col. Abdillahi Yusuf—formerly president of the semi-autonomous north-eastern Somali region of Puntland, based on

83

the Mijerteyn and related Darod clans—who was widely believed to enjoy the strongest financial backing of all candidates.

Abdillahi's candidature was assured by Ethiopian support in a contest where money talked most eloquently. Having enjoyed Ethiopian military assistance, and then custodial hospitality as a prisoner, during his period as SSDF guerrilla leader (or 'terrorist') against Siyad Barre, Abdillahi was no stranger to the new rulers in Addis Ababa. The Ethiopian rulers, likewise, masterminded the appointment of Abdillahi's Prime Minister, Ali Geedi, a Hawiye veterinary professor, who had direct links with the Ethiopian Prime Minister Meles Zenawi, and even less experience of civil politics than Abdillahi. Neither, of course, had any knowledge of democracy in the Western sense, but both supported the new federal constitution which they were charged to implement—at least in theory. Abdillahi was, in fact, quite candid about his own qualifications. In his acceptance speech, he boasted that his nick-name was the 'jackal', that he had fought in every recent Somali war, and could be counted on to continue to fight. Later events, as we shall see, confirmed that this was no idle boast.

Although it spent months hesitating to do so, the resulting 'transitional federal government', with its cabinet and other ministers and members of the assembly, moved back to Somalia in 2005. They did not, however, immediately station themselves at Mogadishu, which was considered too dangerous. They settled first at Jowhar on the Shebelle river, about a hundred miles from Mogadishu, under the protection of Muuse Soodi Yalahow, the prominent (Hawiye) local warlord. When after a few months he and Abdillahi fell out, the TFG nucleus moved to the provincial protection of Baidoa among the Digil Mirifle agro-pastoralists. Though back on Somali soil, the TFG had marginalised itself geographically and politically.

Although it actually had no public electoral mandate, its UN and EU promoters, who largely sustained it financially, vigorously and (suspiciously) repeatedly proclaimed that the TNG was the 'legitimate' (transitional) government of Somalia. But this was definitely not the view of the general Somali public, a significant discrepancy which appeared to be of little or no concern to EU officials and ministers (including the British)—those purportedly seeking to 'democratise' Africa. This curious inconsistency was, of course, partly a reflection of ignorance of the real situation on the ground in Somalia. But it was also a product of a certain deliberate blindness to events that went beyond the simplistic assumptions of the ethnocentric Development bureaucrats who tended to play an increasingly dominant (if questionable) role in European policy towards Africa. When challenged, EU diplomats defended their attachment to their creation, with the curious sophistry that the TFG had to be treated as the legitimate government of Somalia as it was 'the only show in town'!

At home in Somalia, where it was not regarded as a legitimate government, the TFG soon found itself confronting growing public hostility to its claimed status. In fact it completely failed to develop any viable local, and no national administrative organisation and did not restrain, far less control, the criminal activities of its warlord 'ministers' and assemblymen. The latter quickly reverted to type, and even formed their own alternative gang, the CIA-backed coalition grandly named the 'Alliance for the Restoration of Peace and Counter-Terrorism'. From the US perspective, the accent here was naturally on the ubiquitous 'war on terror', and Washington's involvement in this Somali warlord organisation signalled its realistic (if tacit) evaluation of the TFG as a toothless phantom!

Islam brings peace to Mogadishu

The next and, as it turned out, most positive recent development in southern Somalia's wavering quest for governance was the formation of an alliance of Islamic courts, backed by local clan militias. This new phenomenon had been slowly evolving to fill the gap left by the continuing absence of public law and order. This novel, home-grown initiative was also partly provoked by the indiscriminate violence perpetrated by the US-backed 'Counter-terrorism Alliance'. Supported by local clan militias and business interests, the Islamists made security a key issue and turned their guns on the warlords within and outside the 'Alliance'.

Although they were essentially a rather loose and informal collection of local traditional Shariah courts, initially mainly inside Mogadishu, and varied in the degree of fundamentalism of their sheikhs, their cohesion was under-pinned by kin ties within the local Hawiye clans. Professor Said Samatar (2006) aptly described them as a 'rickety amalgam of kinship factions, rather than a single unified Islamic organization, composed of at least eleven separate squabbling groups'. The majority of sheikhs involved were ordinary Somali religious figures, with a few well-known firebrands (such as ex-army colonel Sheikh Hassan Daahir Aways). Some of these activists had links with the Saudi al-Ittihad radicals who were currently enjoying popularity in the Islamic world. Particularly with the memory of their nineteenth century anti-Ethiopian *jihads*, it was hardly necessary to import inspiration specifically from al-Qaida to mobilize Somali religious fervour, especially when it was combined with clan solidarity.

Particularly significant here was the Habar Giddir 'Ayr lineage which, in the shadows of the previous TNG regime of Abdiqasim Salad Hassan, had come to exercise hegemony over a large stretch of southern Somalia, running from Mogadishu through Merca and Brava down to Kismayu. Each of the main Hawiye clans now dominant in southern Somalia had one or more representatives in the Courts Union, which as Said Samatar says, was essentially 'a fragile coalition of clans wrapping themselves in an Islamic flag to make themselves look respectable to the international community and to give the US a fright!'. Especially among the rather unsophisticated locally trained Somali clerics, latent hostility towards non-Muslims, such as the Ethiopians (and by extension the

Americans) regarded as unbelievers, was readily aroused. The associated idea of *jihad* was, in any case, never far in the background. And it soon came to the fore after the courts' initial success in driving the warlords out in six months of action. This was partly certainly a result of their leaders' common kinship links, backed by wide public support. But these early successes tended also to be seen by them as evidence of God's favour for their crusade to extend fundamentalist Islamic law throughout southern Somalia.

This was by no means an easy aim, given that Somalis were generally rather tolerant Muslims. There were, in fact, many issues on which disagreements existed between lay Somalis and the fundamentalist court leaders. Thus, inspired by the Saudi Wahhabis, and like the earlier Somali Dervishes, the latter tended to oppose the local cult of Muslim saints which bulked so large in traditional Somali Islam. They also departed from standard Somali practice in insisting that women should be veiled. Somalis similarly did not normally apply the strict Shariah penalties for crimes which they tended to treat by a tariff of compensation payments.

An especially sensitive issue concerned the well-established Somali practice of chewing the leaves of the *qat* plant for its stimulant properties. When this was summarily outlawed, with those possessing and selling it liable to being lashed with whips and the drug itself seized and burnt, there was considerable public consternation. Similarly, people were astonished when cinema-going, public dancing and singing, and even watching football matches on TV were banned. These were regarded as unjustified attacks on familiar freedoms and provoked hostile criticism. Hence although their political orientation and propaganda against the Ethiopian supporters of Abdillahi Yusuf fitted in well with the public mood at the time, the longer-term popularity of the courts' movement was by no means assured.

Despite these and other unwelcome features, however, this unexpected new religious contribution to the vacuous 'peace process' was generally appreciated. For the first time since the collapse of Somalia in 1991, ordinary citizens found that it was safe to go about their business in the streets of Mogadishu, without fear of attack or molestation. Trade quickly revived, and food prices dropped dramatically. They also benefited from technical and military aid from Eritrea and other sources. With such support, it took only a few weeks for Islamist militias to take over and renovate the main national airport and the seaport—both of which had been under the control of rival warlords and out of action for more than a decade!

None of the many grandiose (but dysfunctional) 'governments' introduced by external intervention, including the latest Kenya-based TFG, had managed to restore public services or security so spectacularly, or indeed to govern at all. The Courts' success was consequently perceived as a serious threat by the Ethiopian government which claimed that this Islamic movement, far from unified though it was, included in its leadership Muslim terrorists who had been implicated in earlier bomb incidents in Ethiopia and Kenya. These charges were reiterated by the Americans, and provided convenient ammunition for the beleaguered TFG leader Abdillahi Yusuf to use in denouncing the Union of Courts with US blessing. The Islamists' hysterical calls for an international Muslim *jihad* against Abdillahi and his Ethiopian and US allies did little, of course, to dimiss the claims that they were 'terrorists'.

By the same token, as US clients, the Ethiopians reinforced their accusations that the sheikhs who ran the Somali Courts were all dangerous terrorists. Ethiopian concern and hostility were also directly intensified by the Courts' appeals for support to the Eritreans and the gamut of opposition fronts inside Ethiopia, especially those which were Muslim or had Islamic links. As, emboldened by their surprisingly easy defeat of the warlords, the Courts began increasingly to menace Abdillahi Yusuf and his TFG holed up in Baidoa, the Ethiopian regime became seriously provoked and started to supply significant military support. The Union of Courts now, inviting Islamic support from all quarters, called for a *jihad* against Abdillahi and his 'infidel' Ethiopian backers, as well as Ethiopia's patrons the Americans. Thus the stage was set for a proxy conflict with the US.

So the essentially domestic dispute over the TFG's legitimacy in Somalia was reconfigured in terms of the US 'war on terror'. The EU, consequently, found its questionable endorsement of the TFG leading into dangerous paths it had never envisaged. By the end of 2006 thousands of Ethiopian troops, tanks and heavy artillery, with air support, were pushing into Somalia. After a few initial battles the Islamists quickly retreated to Mogadishu and then, apparently judging that extended fighting in the city would reduce their public support, withdrew southwards through Kismayu into the Kenyan borderlands. Although they kept well in the background, the Americans showed their hand when, claiming that they were attacking people 'suspected of being terrorists', US warplanes bombed targets which included innocent pastoralist Somalis on the Kenya border. This casual imposition of a collective death sentence showed, by any standards, little respect for law. Observers of the carnage reported that war crimes had been committed and that for complicity in this carnage even EU leaders might be called to account.

After they had taken Mogadishu, the Ethiopian forces, in alliance with detachments of the 'TFG army' (which now included elements from Puntland), nevertheless found their presence challenged by clan and Islamic militias. To deal with this nationalistic resistance, they turned their heavy artillery against the civilian quarters of the city where they believed their opponents were concentrated. Very high rates of civilian casualties ensued, and the wounded were deliberately cut off from medical assistance. As many as half a million civilians are estimated to have fled the holocaust in Mogadishu. By the end of the first week in May 2007, the guns of the local clan militias and Islamic supporters, no match for the sophisticated weapons of the Ethiopian professional forces, fell largely silent and Abdillahi Yusuf declared victory, an-

89

nouncing a series of draconian measures to tame the recalcitrant Hawiye citizens of Mogadishu whom, for political convenience, he called 'Islamists'.

This situation was by no means stable and clearly could not be maintained without the Ethiopian occupation—or, arguably as the UN and others advocated, a replacement force of African 'peace-makers'. The latter, of course, would only be acceptable to Abdillahi Yusuf if this much-misused term was interpreted to mean a support force for the Darod conqueror. Thus the situation in Mogadishu in the early summer of 2007 had significant analogies with that in the late 1980s, before Somalia's collapse in 1990/91, when the Darod military dictator General Muhammad Siyad Barre claimed to rule what was left of Somalia with the support of the Americans, Italy and the UN. This image of dwindling central power became increasingly dominant as the months passed and 2008 began. The so-called insurgents were becoming more expert and dangerous in their guerrilla tactics, with rocket-propelled grenades, land mines, and other deadly equipment, and no lack of external assistance. As well as those associated with the Courts, there were also now well-armed and trained Hawiye youth groups who were becoming more and more daring. Abdillahi and his Ethiopian military allies now ruthlessly applied their heavy weapons to suppress the dwindling population of Hawiye still surviving in Mogadishu, preventing the wounded gaining access to such medical care as was available and cutting off emergency food supplies. Despite the hundreds of thousands of people who fled Mogadishu, making it more and more of a ghost town, deadly guerrilla reprisals continued with murderous incidents every day that showed no sign of letting up.

Partly as a consequence of this level of violent oppression and also of more discerning divide-and-rule tactics, significant changes began to appear in the local clan power structure. The Habar Gidir had lost their political dominance and solidarity, with alterations in the status of such previously dominant lineages as the Saad.

Reflecting on this tragic mess, it is easy to see how once again the process that led to the formation of the TFG had repeated all the major mistakes of previous steps in the circular and unproductive Somalia 'peace process'. The most critical was to fail to insist on the parties actually making peace before trying to make a government. This was the usual denial of the importance of proceeding on a bottom-up basis, with the development of governance as a result of satisfactory peace agreements at the grass roots, instead of proceeding in the reverse top-down direction. These repeated errors probably wasted billions of dollars and caused correspondingly enormous human suffering (cf. A.A. Hirsi 2006 (a and b)). What a pity that in this extraordinary record of material and human destruction, none of the policy leaders was able to recognise and follow the relatively successful experience of state building in the Somaliland Republic.

Together with an unfortunate and unjustifiable attention paid to the vested neo-colonial interests of states like Italy, this is a serious failure on the part of the international community. It is also, of course, a failure on the Somali side where a mixture of jealousy and envy, as well as pride, has prevented southern Somalis from taking the experience of their northern colleagues as a model. Pretending that Somaliland does not actually exist perpetuates their most profound political delusions. It has, unfortunately, no positive result.

4

SOMALILAND AND PUNTLAND

Somaliland: the power of home-made democracy

After it was launched with such enthusiasm by the SNM libera-
tors who recovered Somaliland's freedom in 1991, Somaliland's
initial years were difficult. The construction and financing of an
effective government did not take place overnight. The north was
not immune from the banditry of roving independent militias and
local warlords which ultimately destroyed the south. However, in
January 1993 a 'grand conference of national reconciliation' was
opened at Borama and, over a period of four months, debated
key issues thoroughly, enabling a national consensus to be slowly
developed by the national committee (*gurti*) of 150 elders who
were delegated to vote. An estimated 2,000 people attended and
participated intermittently. Somalis themselves bore most of the
living costs of the representatives, with a little external support.
UNOSOM, committed to a unified Somali state, did not provide
any assistance, despite its proclaimed concern for democracy. Even
more indefensibly, the UN made no contribution to Somaliland's
tough and largely successful demilitarisation programme. Instead
it supported the essentially fantasy demilitarisation campaigns in

Mogadishu, seeking in the absence of government and political order to re-establish a local police force!

The Borama Conference was a critical turning point. Building upon the SNM's original programme, it produced a peace charter (a kind of national *her* treaty) to strengthen basic security and regularise the role and authority of the traditional local elders in all aspects of peace making. It also formulated a national charter to serve for two years as the country's temporary constitution. The new government which Mohamed Haji Ibrahim Egal (former Prime Minister of Somalia) was elected to lead was required to draft a formal constitution, to be put to a national referendum within the two-year period. The most original feature here was an imaginative innovation in the form of a bicameral legislature, with a non-elected upper house of traditional elders (the *gurti)* and an elected lower house of 'representatives'. This arrangement reflected Somali political realities in a way and to an extent that had not previously been tried in the brief political history of Somalia with its Eurocentric political models and focus on so-called 'intellectuals'. It was a sort of compromise between the clan-based SNM (which had provided the military organisation that gained freedom from Siyad Barre) and the exigencies of modern administration. Without doubt, Borama was the centrepiece of these political achievements, lifting Somaliland out of the initial doldrums of its first two 'wasted years' as they have been called.

This striking initiative, in which traditional elders had played such a crucial role (see A.Y. Farah and I.M. Lewis 1994), was repeated in other local peace conferences, notably in Sanag region where the Habar Yunis, Habar Ja'lo, Dulbahante and Warsangeli, traditionally mutually hostile clans, had formed the 'Sanag Grand Peace Conference'. This equally significant assembly, bringing together representatives of Isaq clans with their Darod counterparts (whose territories extended into Darod-based Puntland), concluded in October 1993 with its own regional charter. Of special interest to the local pastoralists and merchants was the charter's provisions for the restoration of traditional reciprocal access to grazing lands, free movement of trade, and return of alienated land. Later, the elders personally supervised the return of land to those who had been displaced during the war.

This is not the place to conduct a detailed comparison of these inexpensive and low-profile Somaliland peace conferences with their extremely expensive, high profile counterparts in Somalia. Here it is simply enough to say that, in general, the former were successful while the latter failed dismally. Of the many factors involved, a crucial difference here is clearly the dominant role played in Somaliland by the local authorities, the 'stake-holders' in the pompous jargon of developers.

With these achievements, the new Isaq President Mohamed Haji Ibrahim Egal, whose lineage and family were from Berbera, was well placed to see that the port of Berbera's revenue was shared nationally. This was all the more important when the Saudi import ban on Somali livestock, imposed to control rinderpest, was lifted and Somaliland's exports resumed. (Unfortunately the ban was reimposed a few years later, and only rescinded again in 2007.) For a few years Berbera was able to challenge the rival port of Djibouti. Following the Ethiopia-Eritrea war and the enduring tensions between these two countries, it gradually developed into a major transit port for Ethiopia, with important economic implications for Somaliland.

These hopeful improvements (which, alas, had no counterpart in Somalia) were accompanied, after the Borama conference, by a vigorous militia demobilisation programme. This led to the re-establishment of the basic structure of government which had collapsed in the 1980s and was not restored by the first SNM administration. Civil servants, now paid regularly, were required to work regular hours. A Planning Ministry was set up, whose work included liaison with foreign NGOs and UN agencies, and the central bank was reopened to administer the new Somaliland shilling as the national currency. Professionally equipped police

95

forces (led by local former officers) were restored in the main towns: Hargeisa, Burao and Borama. There was, however, still a continuing need for effective security.

This priority was highlighted by the setback experienced in late 1994/early 1995 when clan rivalries within the ranks of the Isaq confederation broke into open conflict over the distribution of revenue from the expanding national airport at Hargeisa. Earlier, the local clansmen of Berbera had sought to avoid sharing their local port revenues nationally, and now the airport's local clan attempted to monopolise the revenue from air taxes and landing charges. This issue offered a convenient cause for leading local opponents of President Mohamed Haji Ibrahim Egal and external disaffected Isaq politicians who sought to sabotage Somaliland's struggle for independence from moribund Somalia. Aideed opportunistically took advantage of this conflict, playing a spoiling role by supporting the President's enemies. To its shame, but in character, UNOSOM fostered these divisive moves with encouragement from its political office. With such encouragement, clan fighting soon spread to the commercial town of Burao, where political control had for long been in dispute between the Habar Ja'lo and Habar Yunis clans (both Isaq). Hundreds of thousands of civilians fled, largely to Ethiopia—ironically, the country where they had been refugees earlier, before returning home at the foundation of Somaliland in 1991.

The close ethnic and clan links with the Somali Region, now known in federal Ethiopia as 'Region 5', supplemented by common commercial interests, were reflected in the generally positive attitude of the Ethiopian government towards Somaliland. Indeed this local 'superpower' was the fledgling republic's main external friend.

The UN, as remarked, was disparagingly hostile to these 'nation-building' efforts in Somaliland. Having lost any vestige of neutrality in its clumsy support for the venal centralist Somali politicians, the UN's own aid-coordinating body (safely based, on high personal allowances, in Nairobi, like all its Somalia operations) 'refused to engage constructively with Somaliland and to reinforce principles of good governance and disarmament' (Bradbury 1997).

These adverse developments severely tested the effectiveness of the peace-making resources discussed above. With the cooperation of Somalilanders outside the state, a new Peace Committee for Somaliland was set up; meeting in Ethiopia in the first half of 1996, it managed to restore peace in Burao and Hargeisa. This led to further and wider discussion of the constitution, and although it was controversial, the opportunity was taken to extend Egal's term for a further 18 months, so providing time to end the conflict, to finalise the constitution, and to prepare for elections. On 23 February 1997 Egal was re-elected for another five years, with 223 votes, more than double the number cast for his nearest rival.

But five years later Egal, who had been in poor health for some time, died suddenly in hospital in South Africa. President of Somaliland since 1993 (and before that prime minister of Somalia from 1967 to 1969), Egal was one of the last surviving major Somali civilian leaders. His death inevitably raised concern over Somaliland's future. However, both houses in the Hargeisa parliament voted to follow the constitution and installed the vice-president, Dahir Riyale Kahin. This sensible decision averted a potential constitutional crisis and brought to the presidential office a relatively young and inexperienced politician of the Gadabursi (Dir) clan. As he was outside the dominant Isaq world, his appointment demonstrated that Somaliland had achieved some maturity as a multi-clan and multi-party democratic state: by 2007, with all key political institutions from district councils to the presidency and vice presidency and parliament subject to popular vote, universal suffrage was well established. Somaliland's electoral processes were all closely scrutinised by international observers who reported favourably (see e.g. S. Kibble 2007).

Politics in Somaliland was also closely monitored, and from time to time censured, by Somaliland pressure groups in the UK and USA. When the Somaliland authorities tried to stifle accusations of bribery against leading politicians, including the President, these diaspora groups supported criticism in the local press and censure by opposition members of parliament. Another cause for concern was the Islamic fundamentalist threat that menaced all states in the Horn of Africa. Two serious incidents occurred in October 2003. In the first, on 5 October, a pioneering and widely respected Italian medical volunteer, with many years' experience in Somali communities, was shot by a gunman in the hospital she had founded for tuberculosis and AIDS treatment. In a second incident which raised the old issue of non-Muslims teaching Somalis, two British teachers were shot at the prestigious secondary school in Sheikh. Notwithstanding the sensitivity of the matter, the 'Islamic radicals'—as the police called them—who were held responsible were identified and charged with banditry and terrorism. Here modern Islamic fundamentalism is apt to reinforce unsophisticated traditional prejudice that Christians in general are 'pagans'—not at all the view taken by the learned Muslim judge in the case, who found the culprits guilty of murder.

Although the problems restricting livestock exports to Saudi Arabia were not resolved until 2007, business was thriving and the population had greatly expanded in Hargeisa, which was widely regarded as one of the safest capitals in Africa. New commercial opportunities had developed, attracting young people from the interior whose herding duties were delegated to hired hands from the less prosperous Ogaden. Some indication of these new levels of urban progress was provided by functioning traffic lights on the streets of Hargeisa, as well as traffic police. Another indicator was the opening of popular wedding bureaus (noted by visitors) as well as supermarkets and other modern amenities. There were two universities of similar standard to the old Italian university institute in Mogadishu, and schools were increasing in number and in quality, with by 2007 a UK-sponsored GCE examination board. Health care was slowly improving, spurred on by the impressive Edna Adan maternity hospital, built substantially with the former foreign minister's own funds and with even some direct manual labour by her (as well as, of course, her professional medical expertise).

Despite the difficulties Somaliland faced through its lack of international recognition, it was remarkably successful, both locally and internationally, in the informal economy. Here, in lieu of official banks, the informal money transfer system established throughout the Somali region facilitated the transfer of credit in the form of remittances from most parts of the world. Refugees regularly sent donations, by telephone, from their allowances to their kin at home. Such remittances played a major role in the economies of all the Somali territories, and Somaliland was no exception (for a recent account see Lindley 2007). Thus, connected as it was to world trade through its expanding port of Berbera (used increasingly by Ethiopia), and with more than half a dozen international flights a week, pursuing its own internal democratic progress, Somaliland remained aloof from the farcical circus of 'peace conferences' in Somalia. Still, however, some disappointed former Somaliland politicians forlornly attempted to jump on the endless bandwagon of negotiation in southern Somalia, presenting themselves for political office there as 'representatives' of Somaliland constituencies to which they could not safely return! Inevitably these disgruntled power-hungry individuals acted as would-be spoilers in Somaliland—generally without much success, fortunately. The most sensitive issue remained the status of the Dulbahante and Warsangeli clans in the northeast. Although segments of these Darod clans as well as many of their political leaders were deeply involved in the political processes of Somaliland, their Harti-Darod identity and their colonial experience as volatile border groups made them cast questing glances towards the adjoining part of north-eastern Somalia (Puntland), where they were vulnerable to pressure from their Darod kinsmen, the Mijerteyn.

Puntland and other possibilities

The northeastern promontory of Somalia, occupied by the Mijerteyn Darod clan, was liberated from Siyad's forces by the SSDF in 1991 and immediately launched its own experiment in statecraft on the building block model of Somalia. Having defeated a challenge from al-Ittihad fundamentalists in Bossaso (later to surface again in other parts of Somalia), the SSDF concentrated on establishing a locally self-governing state, based largely on exports (livestock etc.) and imports through its developing port. The restoration of social services was pursued energetically by the SSDF leaders and Mijerteyn intelligentsia who started returning from abroad in considerable numbers. There was, however, a major political problem in that the two principal SSDF leaders could not agree on how to share the spoils of victory. Col. Abdillahi Yusuf, who had led the guerrilla movement, was in competition with General Mohamed Abshir, the widely respected former commander of Somalia's police force. Abdillahi had been detained as a political prisoner in both Siyad's Somalia and Mengistu's Ethiopia. Each was from a rival segment of the Mijerteyn clan, but had wide-ranging support within it. With the traditional clan 'king' (*boqor:* 'King Kong' as he was known) of the powerful Osman Mahamud lineage, they formed what the Swedish anthropologist Bernhard Hellander (1998) described as 'a rudimentary administration for the three Mijertein regions'. As in Somaliland, the lack of formal modern institutions of governance led to an increase in the duties and power of 'traditional' local lineage elders and indeed to a proliferation of such offices throughout the lineage system.

Although they had disposed of the al-Ittihad fundamentalists, the SSDF found themselves confronting a more traditional threat

100

in the shape of the Habar Gidir under Aideed whom they managed, for the moment at least, to prevent from infiltrating their grazing lands. This experience led the SSDF leadership to split into two wings. A military wing under Col. Abdillahi favoured consolidating the recent victory over the Habar Gidir by forming an alliance with the latter; this was opposed by General Mohamed Abshir and the so-called 'intellectual wing' of the SSDF.

While they reached different conclusions, like other Mijerteyn leaders both men sought to conduct their policies in southern Somalia in such as way as to safeguard their continuing clan interests in the well-being of the substantial number of Mijerteyn who had settled in the port and surrounding territory of Kismayu in the far south of Somalia. There was also the consideration that as it was a clan-based entity in the northeast, Puntland's frontier ran through the territories of the Dulbahante and Warsangeli, the two Darod Somaliland clans (belonging with the Mijerteyn to the Harti section) which, in the future, might be claimed, or from which claims might come. Either way, this was an intrinsically problematic boundary, as it had been in colonial times. It was no doubt partly these motives, as well as other considerations such as the ambition of Mijerteyn leaders to participate in the struggle for power in Somalia as a whole, that led the SSDF to refrain from claiming full autonomy for Puntland. The territory was so named in memory of the ancient Egyptian expeditions, in search of rare aromatic gums, to the mystically alluring 'Puntland' (whose location archaeologists dispute). It may be noted that the letter 'p' does not occur in the Somali alphabet and is pronounced 'b' (as in Buntland).

The Puntlanders have always described their region as the 'Puntland state of Somalia', avoiding the clear breach which Somaliland makes. Abdillahi Yusuf succeeded in getting himself elected as Puntland President in March 1998, but this was not accepted by General Mohamed Abshir who had been re-elected SSDF Chairman in January of the same year. The conflict between these two figures was also played out on the wider Somalia political stage where, as we have seen, Col. Abdillahi eventually succeeded in gaining the rather empty crown of transitional federal President. Puntland seemed to remain in his eyes as a kind of bolt-hole where, in the event of things going wrong in Mogadishu, he might hope to find refuge.

In Puntland as in Somaliland, the lack of formal modern institutions of governance had led to an increase in the number of 'traditional' local lineage heads, and indeed to a rich burgeoning of lineage 'chiefs', known collectively as *issmo,* throughout the lineage system. This over-production of formal political dignitaries inevitably led to a reduction in the status of the office. Sociologically, it seemed to indicate a reversion of political solidarity to lower levels in the system, detracting from the potential wider solidarity at clan level. This is what might be expected under the general conditions of Puntland at large, when the Mijerteyn were no longer fully mobilized for wider conflicts, and internal politics were in a state of confusion. Much the same, as we have seen, had occurred in Somaliland.

Col. Abdillahi's tenure of the presidency expired in June 2001, and following the provisional charter, the Chief Justice took the helm temporarily and began organising a conference to elect the new president and vice-president. In the meantime, Colonel Abdillahi created astonishment by stepping in himself and proclaimed that he was president with a new mandate for three more years. This mandate, he claimed, had been issued by the now defunct parliament; public funds had been openly used to bribe members of parliament and of the armed forces to maintain him in power. Arguments on the legality of Abdillahi's actions became increasingly heated, and the traditional clan leaders intervened, summoning a week-long meeting at Garowe to which Abdillahi, his Vice President and the Chief Justice were invited. The traditional leaders requested the outgoing presidential team to transfer Puntland's sovereignty to them. Yusuf and his deputy rejected this request and reiterated their clams to legitimacy. The rebuffed traditional leaders took extensive legal advice which only served to convince them of the correctness of their position. The Chief Justice was accordingly invited to commence a thirty-day period as caretaker president, and to prepare for an election conference to take place in August 2001.

Col. Abdillahi, however, stubbornly maintained that he was still in charge, and mustering a force of his supporters, personally led an attack on Bossaso airport on 5 August. On the next day, the local population rose angrily against this illegal intrusion and defeated Abdillahi and his followers who retreated to Garowe and finally to Galkayu where he was again publicly rejected. His next move was to announce on the BBC Somali service that he had been thrown out of office by Islamic extremists, thus harking back to his earlier exploits against al-Ittihad! This claim. as was perhaps intended, aroused Ethiopian (as well as US) interest, securing for the renegade ex-President a fresh influx of military aid from his Ethiopian allies.

Meanwhile, by 22 August, the chief justice who was caretaker President, with the support of the traditional elders was busy preparing for the conference planned to select the new president. A grand conference of delegates to carry out this process was convened and eventually, on 14 November, elected Jama Ali Jama as the new president who was sworn in on the following day. A week later, the indomitable colonel, and his supporting forces, launched a mortar attack on the residences of the chief justice, and the new president, who were fortunate to escape with their lives. In 2002, Abdillahi wrested control from his rivals and held on to the position until he was at last replaced by Mahamud Muse Adde, elected by due process in 2005. By this time, Abdillahi's soaring ambitions had found the summit of success in his appointment as president of Somalia's 'transitional federal government'. He could still hope to exercise significant influence in Puntland through Somalia's theoretically federal constitution.

It goes without saying that the new Puntland president, Mahamud Muse Adde, was to continue to have complicated relations with his forceful predecessor who routinely interfered in Puntland's local affairs. The state was in fact constitutionally lop-sided in that the presidency was strong but the local assembly weak, a situation owing much to Abdillahi Yusuf's dictatorial rule. It also probably reflected the constitutional contrast with Somaliland's bicameral system where the upper house of traditional dignitaries acted as a brake on the lower house of elected party representatives. Puntland had no second chamber and no parties, making it easier for the president to act autocratically in disregard of his sixty-six member House of Representatives.

In 2007, however, Puntland appeared to be beset with problems, bringing the political tensions between these rival centres of power into sharp relief. In most cases these involved the presidency attempting to act independently of parliament or in defiance of it. Most of these difficulties reflected the declining economy of the country. In the first quarter of the year, an attempt was made by the Puntland authorities to solve the perennial problem of illegal off-shore fishing by unusually vigorous policing. Fishing boats of many different nations regularly traversed these waters, and were frequently stopped and captured by Puntlanders on high speed gunboats (the maritime equivalent of the famous terrestrial 'technicals'). It was generally claimed that the fishermen concerned had no licences. But some local commentators alleged that they did have legitimate permits and were being doubly exploited by agents of those who had originally issued permits. By no means all the 'illegal' fishermen were from Yemen, but many were and the new Puntland police vigilance led to difficulties with Yemen and a move to regularise matters. Eventually, agreement was reached with Yemen over fishing rights, and on the more poignant issue of control of human trafficking. Here large numbers of southern Somali asylum seekers sought refuge in Yemen as passengers on small, over-crowded dhows with a high death toll. Abdillahi

Yusuf's TFG objected to these third party agreements claiming that Puntland lacked the power to treat directly with Yemen. This intervention brought a sharp and interesting retort from Puntland's fishing minister. He stated that Puntland owned its coastal resources and would continue to do so until a referendum was held on federalism and decided otherwise.

A more puzzling episode, noted in the international press, occurred in early June when a US warship bombarded the hills surrounding the small port of Bargal. Locally it was reported that a group of 'Islamists', presumed to be connected with al-Qaida, had landed in the region on the north-east Puntland coast and attacked the local police. Since Puntland forces were also apparently involved, this operation was evidently authorized by the local authorities who seemed to have as good lines of communication with US agents as Abdillahi Yusuf himself enjoyed.

Similarly evoking such contradictions between federal and local interests, president Mahamud Adde had earlier granted an Arabian company exclusive rights, for a fifteen year period, to export Puntland livestock—despite opposition from local business interests and parliamentary dissent. Illegal fishing and local responses to it were in any case part of a much more serious and financially rewarding problem: the growing prevalence of commercial piracy and hostage-taking off the Puntland coast. This had a long history. In the nineteenth century, the loot from coastal shipwrecks (sometimes apparently induced by misleading navigational advice from the coast) was a significant element in the Mijerteyn trading economy, organized by the traditional leaders, and may even have contributed to centralizing tendencies in the power structure of the local sultanates. Here, as in so many facets of modern Somali life, there is much essential continuity between past and present.

More immediately, Puntland's hyper-inflation was causing basic problems which the Mahamud Adde administration was evidently unable to remedy. Amid suspicions and accusations that the government was printing counterfeit currency to pay civil servants, there were strikes and protests in Bossaso and Garowe, and finance became a major issue between the administration and parliament which, in July 2007, sent back the 2006 budget review without passing it. The ministry of finance and the presidency had been given more funds than the sum allocated by parliament, whereas the ministries of health and interior, as well as the security services, had not received their allocated budgets.   Pressed to appear before the legislature to answer members' questions about his failing policies, Mahamud Adde ignored these requests and sought evasive action. He claimed unconvincingly that he was being undermined by the anti-TFG political opposition based in Eritrea which was, he alleged, in alliance with the Somalilanders. In June, however, accompanied by several of his ministers, he did finally appear before parliament where he was closely questioned on the counterfeit currency allegations until the speaker intervened to close the session prematurely.

At the end of July, popular dissent led to riots in the streets of Garowe with pedestrians stoning the president. At this time, either coincidentally or with remarkable timing, a Somaliland delegation visited parts of Sool region claimed by Puntland. This prompted the Puntland authorities to seek help from Abdillahi Yusuf who had already himself received help from home in the form of several thousand Puntland soldiers. These it was announced were now to be incorporated in the official TFG forces and would benefit by receiving pay, uniforms, and other equipment. The main point of their formal attachment to the TFG president was, of course, that this gave some substance to his claim to have national soldiery at his disposal in addition to the Ethiopian detachments sent to assist him in his hour of need in Somalia.

While the decade had begun with the invasion by Puntland forces of Dulbahante and other Darod areas in Somalland, it seemed to be ending with the re-emergence in these disputed districts of a return to Somaliland allegiance. This optional loyalty was apparently now perceived as bringing more tangible gains in administrative services and development prospects Although it had its own administrative difficulties, Somaliland was functionally a more impressive enterprise than Puntland which, after all, was the end of the line in the deeply compromised state of Somalia. Such prominence as the latter enjoyed was ephemeral and depended on the accident that, for the time being, Somalia's nominal president (Abdillahi Yusuf) was a Puntlander (see also Hoehne, 2007). Thus Puntland tied its destiny (through common clanship) to the disfunctional wreck of Somalia. How beneficial this would prove in the long term was problematic, especially considering the delicate medical condition of the TFG president Abdillahi Yusuf, as an elderly, if very energetic person with a liver transplant.

These uncertainties particularly affected local political life in the Darod centres of Somaliland where the attractions of Puntland waned and waxed unpredictably. Like Somalis generally, with their acute experience of the precariousness of life as pastoral nomads, political commitments and loyalties see-sawed with dramatic variability in the Darod borderland and the local political game, where prominent political figures could be found in high positions on either side of the border, was to maximize these shifting opportunities as advantageously as possible.

Within southern Somalia, the next in line to achieve local federal autonomy was probably the 'South Central Region' (Bay and Bakol) of the Digil Mirifle agro-pastoralists. This had been established by the Rahanweyn Resistance Army led originally by the colourful guerrilla commander 'Sharti Gudud' (literally 'Red Shirt').With Ethiopian assistance he had liberated his Digil Mirifle region from the Hawiye militias who had seized control in the earlier 1990s. In 2007, a university was announced to be under formation at Baidoa. Meanwhile, this and many other projects had a strongly aspirational quality, since despite the repetitious EU polemics about Somalia's s 'federal institutions',[2] these would

---

2   On the background to these federal developments see I.M. Lewis and J. Mayall (eds), *A Study of Decentralised Political Structures for Somalia,*

have no effective legal status until a national referendum actually took place and endorsed this exotic concept. How federalism, if implemented in practice, would be articulated in whatever was then left of Somalia was a matter for speculation. Nor was it easy to foresee what impact such developments might have on Puntland and Somaliland.

London: LSE, 1995.

APPENDIX 1

SOMALI CLAN FAMILIES

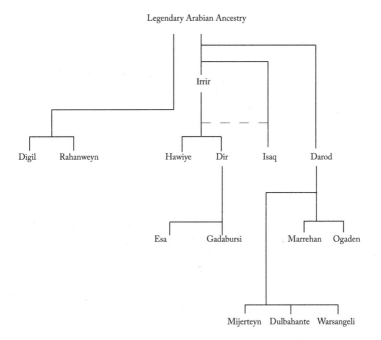

Legendary Arabian Ancestry

Irrir

Digil   Rahanweyn   Hawiye   Dir   Isaq   Darod

Esa   Gadabursi   Marrehan   Ogaden

Mijerteyn   Dulbahante   Warsangeli

'Pastoralists": DIR, ISAQ, HAWIYE: DAROD (descended from legendary remote common ancestor 'Samale'
'Southern Agro-pastoralists': RAHANWEYN (also known as 'Reweyn' and 'Digil Mirifle', from common legendary ancestor 'Mirifle') and DIGIL. (Both known collectively as descendants of legendary ancestor 'Sab')

* These occupational descriptions are approximate since, in practice 'Samale' are found in both categories, as well as among urbanised towns-people.

APPENDIX 2

REFERENCES AND SUGGESTED READING

Some of the references that appeared in the earlier edition have been retained for their importance to the subject. But they will only be obtainable from libraries. The documentation here of their sometime existence is for the benefit of present and future researchers and others interested in more extensive study. A number of recent publications, which are considered of little serious value, have been excluded deliberately.

General ethnograhic features /traditional culture

A.A. Abokor, *The Camel in Somali Oral Traditions*, Uppsala: Scandinavian Institute of African Studies, 1987.

B.W. Andrzejewski and I.M. Lewis, *Somali Poetry*, Oxford, 1964. Following an outline of the socio-cultural setting, this book for the first time displayed to European readers the riches of Somali oral poetry through texts and translations.

B.W. Andrzejewski with S. Andrzejewski, *An Anthology of Somali Poetry*, Bloomington: Indiana University Press, 1993. A collection of Somali poetry, translated by B.W. Andrzejewski and his wife.

Richard Burton's *First Footsteps in East Africa*, recording the author's expedition from Zeila to Harar in 1854, first published in 1856 (continued in print ever since), remains a vivid and accurate account of many features of traditinal Somali culture.

John Wm. Johnson's *"HEELLOY": Modern Poetry and Songs of the Somali*, London: Haan, 1996, shows how contemporary popular poetry cast in the idiom of love songs offers a lively political commentary on events. With some poems in both Somali and English, and a foreword by Abdilahi Qarshe, a legendary exponent of the genre.

Johnson, J. *et al.*, *Somalia in Word and Image*, Washington DC: Foundation for Cross Cultural Understanding, 1986. Produced to accompany an ethnographic collection on Somalia, this contains essays by established scholars, and a wealth of information on artistic and cultural expression among the range of Somali groups.

I.M. Lewis, *Peoples of the Horn of Africa*, London: International African Institute, 1955 and 1969; re-published by Haan Associates 1993; fourth edn. 1998: provides a detailed picture of Somali life, social institutions and general culture. It also contains an exhaustive (up to 1960) bibliography. The book is based on a survey of sources published prior to 1954, and, except for an appendix 'Population and Land Use in the Somali Inter-riverine Areas' (pp.199-222), does not include the results of its author's own fieldwork begun in 1955. Extensive use is made of the pioneering studies of the great Italian scholars Enrico Cerulli and Massimo Colucci. The former's collected works on Somalia were reprinted in three volumes, and published in Rome in 1957 and 1959 with the title *Somalia: scritti vari editi ed inediti.*

S.S. Samatar, *Oral Poetry and Somali Nationalism*, Cambridge University Press, 1982. A brilliant study by the Professor of African History at Rutgers University of the crucial role of poetry in Somali politics, especially in the case of the Somali *jihad* leader Sayyid Muhammad Abdille Hassan.

Lee V. Cassanelli, 'Qat: Changes in the Production and Consumption of a Quasilegal Commodity in Northeast Africa', in A. Appadurai (ed.), *The Social Life of Things*, Cambridge University Press, 1986. One of the most useful accounts of the socio-economics of the consumption of the stimulant leaves (containing ephedrine) of the *qat* plant. These are increasingly chewed by men (and some women) throughout the Somali region. They have a debilitating effect and their consumption causes a serious drain on family budgets.

Pastoral nomadism: resources, and nomadic organisation

A.M. Abdullahi, *Pastoral Production Systems in Africa: a Study of Nomadic Household Economy and Livestock Marketing in Central Somalia*, Kiel: Wissenschaftsverlag Vauk, 1990.

D.R. Aronson, 'Kinsmen and Comrades: towards a Class Analysis of the Somali Pastoral Sector', *Nomadic Peoples*, No. 7, November 1980, pp. 14-24, examines the profits being made by middlemen and large-scale stock exporters.

J.A. Hunt's *A General Survey of the Somaliland Protectorate, 1944-50*, London: Crown Agents, 1957, provides excellent detailed information on the physical environment, and seasonal pastoral movements.

I.M. Lewis's *A Pastoral Democracy*, London: International African Institute, 1961 (new edition with preface by Said Samatar and afterword by the author, Oxford: James Currey, 1999) is a detailed social anthropological analysis of northern Somali nomadism and politics in the late 1950s. It includes material on the cultivators in the northwest, and on a religious settlement, as well as an account of the foundation of modern Somali political parties and nationalism.

I.M. Lewis, *Blood and Bone: the Call of Kinship in Somali Society*, Trenton, NJ: Red Sea Press, 1993. This book brings together related studies of different aspects of Somali kinship ideology and behaviour in northern and southern Somalia. It explores how Somalis use kinship as a 'natural' vehicle for all forms of joint interest, economic as well as political. The last three chapters examine post-independence politics at the 'national' level, including 'Scientific Socialism' in Somalia, and the foundation of the Somaliland Republic.

For further detailed analysis of subsequent political developments in Somalia and Somaliland, see I.M.Lewis, *Making and Breaking States in the Horn of Africa: the Somali experience*, Trenton, NJ, Red Sea Press, 2008.

Jama Mohamed, 'Kinship and Contract in Somali Politics', *Africa* vol. 77, no. 2, 2007, pp. 226-49. This highly original article by the brilliant young Somali historian argues persuasively that by privileging the principle of blood kinship and clan identity (*tol*) over that of contractual agreement (*xer*), modern Somali politicians adopted a divisive rhetoric which undermined wider political cohesion. The author is undoubtedly the foremost historical scholar of his generation in the field of Somali Studies.

J. Swift, 'Pastoral Development in Somalia' in M.H. Glantz (ed.), *Desertification: Environmental Degradation in and around Arid Lands*, Boulder, CO: Westview Press, 1977 contains some interesting speculations on socio-economic change among the northern nomads

Southern agricultural Somalis

[The best general sociological analysis here is still M. Colucci's *Principi di diritto Consuetudinario della Somalia italiana meridionale*, Florence 1924, but it is extremely rare, even in academic libraries]

The key modern social anthropological study of a southern Rahanweyn Somali tribe is B. Helander's *The Slaughtered Camel; Coping with Fictitious Descent among the Hubeer of Southern Somalia*, University of Uppsala, 2003.

A recent and very readable account of southern Somali groups from the Afgoi area is V. Luling's detailed study *Somali Sultanate: the Geledi City-state over 150 Years*, London: Haan, 2002. Includes a description of the famous 'stick-fight' ritual.

G. Massey, *Subsistence and Change: Lessons of Agropastoralism in Somalia*, Boulder, CO: Westview Press, 1987. A valuable survey study of village production in southern Somalia.

Southern urban traditions

E.A. Alpers has written a number of interesting articles on urban life in southern Somalia, including 'Muqdisho in the 19th Century: A Regional Perspective', *Journal of African History* vol. 24, 1983, pp. 441–59, and 'Futa Benaadir: Continuity and Change in the Traditional Cotton Textile Industry of Southern Somalia' in C. Coquéry-Vidrovitch (ed.), *Entreprises et Entrepreneurs en Afrique aux 19me et 20me siècles*, Paris: Harmattan, 1983.

Reese, Scott S., 'Patricians of the Benaadir: Islamic Learning, Commerce and Somali Urban Identity in the Nineteenth Century', University of Pennsylvania: Unpublished thesis, 1996.

Scikei, Nuredin Hagi, *Banaadiri: The Renewal of a Millenary Identity*, Bologna: CLUEB, 2002. This is a delightful introduction to the architecture of the Benadir port towns, and a welcome addition to literature on a little documented subject.

Islam

Said S. Samatar (ed.), *In the Shadow of Conquest: Islam in Colonial Northeast Africa*, Trenton, NJ: Red Sea Press, 1992, contains two of his own chapters (one on Sh. Uways of Brava and the general introduction) with other chapters on Sh. Zayla'i, and on the Salihiya and Sayyid Muhumad Abdille Hassan. Other chapters deal with Islam and resistance in Wallo, Gondar and the Sudan.

Saints and Somalis: Popular Islam in a Clan-based Society, London: Haan, 1998 is a collection of essays by I.M. Lewis that explores the central place and role of Islam among the Somali people.

Brad Martin's *Muslim Brotherhoods in 19th-Century Africa*, Cambridge University Press, 1976 devotes two chapters to Sufi Brotherhoods in Somalia.

Trimingham, J.S., *Islam in Ethiopia*, London: Frank Cass, 1965. Will be found in libraries. This is more accurately about Islam in the Horn of Africa, and contains many references to Islamic traditions among Somalis.

Settlement schemes for nomads

J.M. Haakonsen, *Scientific Socialism and Self-Reliance*, 1984 provides interesting information on the fishing co-operatives, based on a short preliminary study.

R. Antoniotto, 'The Fishing Settlement at Baraawe: Notes on Cultural Adaptation', in *Somalia and the World: Proceedings of the International Symposium*, Mogadishu: National Printing Press, 1979, Vol. 2, pp. 237-50; E. Forni, `Woman's New Role and Status in the Baraawe Settlement' in ibid., pp. 251-65 provide some documentation on the fishing settlement at Brava.

History (see also Pastoral nomadism)

N. Chittick, 'An Archaeological Reconnaissance in the Horn: The British-Somali Expedition, 1975', Azania, Vol. XI, 1976, pp. 117-33, provides a rare and indispensable survey of the current archaeological situation in Somalia

L. V. Cassanelli, *The Shaping of Somali Society: Reconstructing the History of a Pastoral People, 1600-1900*, Philadelphia: University of

Pennsylvania Press, 1982. Based on oral and written sources, this is a pioneering study of southern Somalia over three centuries.

Neville Chittick, 'Early Ports in the Horn of Africa', *Journal of Nautical Archaeology and Underwater Exploration*, vol. 8 no. 4, 1979, pp. 273-7.

—— 'Medieval Mogadishu' in *From Zinj to Zanzibar, Studies in History, Trade and Society on the Coast of Eastern Africa*, Frankfurt-am-Main: Frobenius Institute, 1982.

Ali Abdirahman Hirsi's 'The Arab Factor in Somali History' (Unpublished PhD thesis, University of California, Los Angeles, 1977) provides a unique analysis of the Arabian connection in Somalia, making extensive use of previously neglected Arabic sources. Dr Ali has also written penetrating assessments, partly based on his own direct participation in the 'Arta' provisional government, of the disastrous failure of the latest attempts to cobble together governments in Somalia. He exposes the crucial misunderstanding, shared by the international community, that viable government could be restored without those involved first engaging in effective reconciliation. Dr Ali's articles are at the time of writing only available on the internet, but they are so valuable they are well worth tracing. See wardheernews.com/ Articles 06-29/06/2006 Somalia Governance.Crisis

J. Drysdale, *The Somali Dispute*, London: Pall Mall and New York: Frederick A. Praeger, 1964; a standard work on the pan-Somali issue. On later developments inside Somalia, from the perspective of a policy adviser in the field, see the same author's *Whatever Happened to Somalia*, London: Haan, 1994, and *Stoics without Pillows*, Haan 2000.

R.L. Hess's *Italian Colonialism in Somalia*, University of Chicago Press, 1966, provides a useful history of Italian rule in pre-independence Somalia.

D. Laitin and S.S. Samatar, *Somalia: Nation in Search of a State*, Boulder, CO: Westview Press, 1987. A valuable general account of Somali history, especially since independence in 1960.

Mohamed Osman Omar, *The Road to Zero: Somalia's Self-destruction*, London: Haan, 1992. A 'life and times' social history account of the period from the 1950s to the overthrow of Siyad Barre by a former chief of protocol and diplomat.

A.I. Samatar, *Socialist Somalia: Rhetoric and Reality*, London: Zed, 1988. An assessment of the 'socialist' era in Somalia.

115

Africa Watch, *Somalia: A Government at War with its Own People*, London, 1990. A 'human rights' perspective of Siyad's campaigns against the population of northern Somalia.

A. Sheikh-Abdi, *Divine Madness: Mohammed Abdulle Hassan (1856-1920)*, London: Zed, 1993. A new evaluation of the Seyyid, including some previously untranslated poetry.

I.M. Lewis's *A Modern History of the Somali: Nation and State in the Horn of Africa*, Oxford: James Currey, 2002 is the standard political history of Somali affairs from pre- to post-independence.

Somalia's collapse and post-1990 developments

I.M. Lewis and J. Mayall (eds), *A Study of Decentralised Political Structures for Somalia*, London: LSE, 1995. The fruits of an LSE study and conference organised for the EC. This seems to have had some influence on the 2005/6 EC-sponsored attempt to restore governance in Somalia.

Drawing on evidence of disputes over land rights and natural resources extending over several decades, a collection of essays, *The Struggle For Land In Southern Somalia: The War Behind The War*, edited by C. Besteman and L.V. Cassanelli, London: Haan and Boulder, CO: Westview, 1996 adds to the understanding of contemporary factional politics and ethnic/regional rivalries in Somalia.

Somalia: Economy without State, Oxford: James Currey, 2003 by Peter D. Little examines the success of the informal Somali economy unhindered by state organisation. No surprise to anthropologists but less familiar to economists and developers.

J. Gardner and J. El Bushra' (eds), *Somalia, The Untold Story: The War through the Eyes of Somali Women*, London: Pluto Press, 2004.

The Somali Remittance Sector in Canada: a Comprehensive Account of How the 'Hawala' System Works in Somalia, and the Main 'Hawala' Agencies, Buri M. Hamza, (York University, Canada, 2006).

Ahmed Yusuf Farah, *Somalia: the Roots of Reconciliation: Peace-making in the Grassroots Peace Conferences of Somaliland*. London: Actionaid, 1993.

M. Bradbury, *Somaliland: Country Report*, London: Catholic Institute for International Relations, 1997. A useful account of the formation and early years of this new country up to the date of publication. Includes an extensive list of NGO reports.

M.Hoene, 'From pastoral to state politics: Traditional authorities in Northern Somalia. In Buur,L. and Kyed,H.M.(eds) *A New Dawn for traditional authorities? State recognition and democratization in sub-Saharan Africa* ,New York, Palgrave, 2007, pp.155-182.

Anna Lindley, 'Remittances to Hargeisa from the Diaspora', *Journal of the Anglo-Somali Society*, no. 41, Spring 2007, pp. 26-30.

Steve Kibble, 'Somalia/Somaliland: Territory, State and Nation', a valuable account of Somaliland's new institutions and elections by a development worker for Progressio involved as an election observer in Somaliland. Talk given at Kings College, London, 13 February 2007.

An illuminatinating report for policy makers and service providers about the Somali community in the UK is Hermione Harris, *The Somali Community in the UK: What We Know and How We Know it* (Information Centre about Asylum and Refugees in the UK, King's College London, June 2004).

Issa-Salwe's *The Collapse of the Somali State: The Impact of the Colonial Legacy*, London: Haan, 1996 is a modern Somali history from an inside perspective. With explorations of the southern Somalia sultanates, and a useful reference section. Isse-Salwe has also produced a major study of the use and importance of the Internet in contemporary Somali life, especially in relation to politics: 'Electronic Communication and an Oral Culture: The political Dynamics of Somali Websites and Mailing Lists', PhD thesis, Thames Valley University, November 2006.

M.H. Mukhtar, 'The Plight of the Agro-pastoral Society of Somalia', *Review of African Political Economy*, Vol. 32, No. 7, pp. 543-53. An important historical contribution from a social scientist from the region in question.

Extensive research projects by WSP International in partnership with local institutions has produced 'road maps' for regeneration in Puntland and in Somaliland: *Rebuilding Somalia: Issues & Possibilities for Puntland*, London: Haan 2001, and *Rebuilding Somaliland: Issues and Possibilities*, RSP, 2005.

The following are specifically written with asylum seekers in mind:

Minority Groups in Somalia, Joint British, Danish and Dutch fact-finding mission to Nairobi, Kenya, Sept. 2000.

Lee Cassanelli, *Victims and Vulnerable Groups In Southern Somalia*, Ottawa: Immigration and Refugee Board, Canada, 1995.

On the Bantu-Somalis, see D. Van Lehman and O. Eno, *The Somali Bantu: their History and Culture*, Washington DC, 2003, prepared as background to help social workers and others with the resettlement of Bantu refugees in America.

Novels

The most successful modern Somali novelist writing in English is Nuruddin Farah. The following are some of his many titles: *From a Crooked Rib*, 1970 (his first novel); *A Naked Needle*, 1976 (a view of contemporary Mogadishu); *Sweet and Sour Milk,* 1980 (set in mid-1970s Somalia); *Maps*, winner of the Neustadt International Prize for Literature in 1998; *Knots*, 2007.

Mahmood Gaildon, *Yibir of Las Burgabo*, Trenton, NJ: Red Sea Press, 2005 is a timely story of a family from one of Somalia's 'outcast' groups and a young man's search for social acceptance.

Marion Molteno, *A Shield of Coolest Air*, London: Shola Books, 1992 is about Somali refugee families in the UK.

Abdirazak Y. Osman, *In the Name of Our Fathers*, London: Haan, 1997 is a first novel, set in the tumultuous days of the fall of a dictator and the collapse of a society into chaos, echoing the experiences of ordinary families whose lives were forever changed by the events of 1991 in Somalia.

Language and linguistics

Husseyn M. Adam's Master's thesis 'A Nation in Search of a Script', Makerere University, 1969 recounts the problems involved in choosing a script for Somali.

The leading international authority on Somali linguistics was the late B.W. Andrzejewski of the SOAS, London, whose work can be found with reference to academic linguistic journal publications. A useful introduction is R.J. Hayward and I.M. Lewis (eds), *Voice and Power: the Culture of Language in North-East Africa. Essays in Honour of B.W. Andrzejewski,* London: SOAS, 1996.

David D. Laitin's *Politics, Language and Thought*, University of Chicago Press, 1977 explores the relationship between Somali ethnic identity and the use of the national language as oral and written medium.

M.M. Moreno, *Il Somalo della Somalia,* Rome: Istituto Poligrafico dello Stato, 1955.

Omar Osman Mohamed's *From Written Somali to a Rural Development Campaign,* Mogadishu: SIDAM, 1975 recounts the successful literacy campaigns using the Latin script, adopted by the Siyad Barre government in 1972.

The best introduction to the Somali language for English speakers is *Colloquial Somali: The Complete Course for Beginners,* by Martin Orwin of the SOAS, London: Routledge, 1995, with cassettes to accompany the course.

For those who can read Somali, the highly original works of the self-taught Somali historian Sheikh Aw Jama Umar Ise are especially important for the Dervish period (1900-1920). See also Y.I. Kenadiid, *Ina Abdille Hassan,* 1984.

The American State Department's *Area Handbook* is a useful wide-ranging source of information.

The *Anglo-Somali Society Journal* is published twice a year and regularly contains interesting articles.

Two international journals specialise in Somali Studies and the Horn of Africa:

Horn of Africa: an Independent Journal, ed. Professor S.S. Samatar, History Department, Rutgers University, 329 Conklin Hall, 175 University Avenue, Newark, NJ 07102. Email:hornofafrica@ rutgers.edu

Bildhaan: an International Journal of Somali Studies, ed. Ahmed I. Samatar, Macalester College, International Studies and Program-

119

ming, 1600 Grand Avenue, St Paul, MN 55105 Email: bild-haan@macalster.edu

For current information on the internet there are scores of Somali internet sites, all of which are editorially partisan but carry news and comment from a range of sources; other useful online sites are the UN IRIN news network and the BBC news networks. Periodic and annual situation reports are produced by UN agencies such as UNHCR and OCHA, and by non-governmental human rights organisations such as Africa Watch and Amnesty International. A Somali NGO that has acquired a reputation for its unbiased reporting is the Dr Ismail Jimale Human Rights Organisation (DIJHRO).

Wikipedia, the free online encyclopaedia, contains information of variable accuracy.

GLOSSARY OF TERMS

Conventional Anglicised spelling of the Somali word is used in some instances to assist the reader who is unfamiliar with the Somali orthography to achieve a close approximation of the pronounciation.

'aano (caano)	milk
adi	sheep and goats (collective term)
Af-maymay	dialect spoken by Digil and Rahanweyn
aqal	collapsible nomad's tent
ardaa wadag	camel herdsmen's communal sleeping mat
aros (aroos)	marriage house
bah	uterine family
bahweyn/minweyn	senior wife
baraka	religious power posessed by religious leaders and teachers, and believed by Somalis to be inherited as well as achieved
bariis	rice
barkad	cement-lined water tank
bildan/billed/bullo	villages
buri	tobacco
burnuq	sweet potatoes
bu'ur	squashes
dangalo	co-wife/jealousy
darab	measure of cultivated land
dayr	autumn
degmo	grazing encampment (from deg: to settle)
diir/digir	beans
diya	blood compensation (also mag)
dumaal	widow inheritance
gel (geel)	camels
gelay	maize
guri	nomad domestic group (from gur: to move)
gu'	spring (season)
guudv	hairstyle of Gaaljecel and Garre clansmen
haas/raas (xaas)	uterine family
haasas/ raasas (xaasas)	polygynous family
heer (xeer)	treaty, contract
heerka qoyska (xeerka)	family law

hiddid (xiddid)	ties established by marriage
higsisan (xigsiisan)	replacement wife (for widower)
jaalle	friend, comrade (N.B. This word became so inextricably associated with the most hated aspects of the Barre regime that it has lost acceptable usage.)
qassab	sugarcane
kewawa	heavy blunt wooden rake used in cultivation
laws (loows)	groundnuts
mahar (meher)	witnessed marriage contract
mal (maal)	capital (particularly livestock)
misego	sorghum
mod	disposable wealth
moos	squares of cultivated land (2m x 2m)
muus	bananas
mundille	mud and wattle hut
Nabad-doon	peace-seekers
oday(al)	elder(s) (also 'duk' and 'akhyaar')
qatv	*catha edulis*: the leaves of this plant, imported in bundles from Kenya and Ethiopia, which looks like an English privet hedge, and chewed for their stimulant properties.
qabila	clan (Arabic)
reer	group, people
reer guura	gazing camel units (i.e. nomads)
saar	spirit possession illness (mainly in women)
simsim	sesame
sonkorqan	sweet potatoes
sultan(s)/ suldhaan(o)	dynastic head (also 'ugas', 'gerad', 'boqor')
suf (suuf)	cotton
tima adag	agricultural serfs, literally 'coarse-haired'
tol	clan descent (hence 'tolayn', nationalisation)
ul	40 or 50 'moos' (measure of land)
'urad (curad)	first-born children
wadad(s)/ waddaad(o)	shiekh(s), religious leader(s), teacher(s)
war	artificial pond used by nomads and cultivators
yambo	hand-hoe
yarad	marriage payments from groom's to wife's group

APPENDIX 3

CHRONOLOGY

This outline is based on written documentary material and excludes the earlier 'pre-history' of the region.

9/10th C AD	Arab families settled in ports along the Somali coast, spreading Islam.
12th C AD	Northern Somali clans spread southwards (having probably fanned out into the Horn from an earlier movement northwards in the first millenium AD)
14th C	Arab traveller Ibn Batuta provides vivid contemporary descriptions of life in the towns of Zeila and Mogadishu.
1540/1560	First detailed reference in written chronicles to Somali people and component clans during the time of the great Muslim champion, Ahmed Gurey (Gran), leader of *jihad* against the Christian Ethiopian kingdom. Somali warriors in his forces described as being especially expert at road ambushes.
17th century	Inhabitants of coastal town of Mogadishu, with predominant Arab and Persian influence, under pressure from Hawiye Somali (Abgal) of the hinterland, who settled in Shangani quarter of the city. This was followed by a period of Omani influence along the southern Somali coast.
1848	French explorer Charles Guillain visited southern Somali ports and immediate hinterland, providing excellent descriptions of the local political situation.

1854	In the course of his famous expedition to the Muslim city state of Harar on the edge of the Ethiopian escarpment, British Arabist and explorer Richard Burton spent several months on the northern Somali coast, between Berbera and Zeila. His *First Footsteps in East Africa* contains detailed and accurate information on Somali culture in this period. Burton memorably describes Somalis as a 'fierce and turbulent race of republicans'.
1897	Imperial partition of the Somali nation. Following the short-lived Egyptian colonisation of the northern Somali coast, Britain, France and Italy signed 'protection' treaties with various Somali clans and partitioned the whole area with Ethiopia.
1920-1920	Sayyid Mohamed Abdille Hassan (the 'Mad Mullah') led a holy war against 'infidel' colonisers—especially Ethiopians and British.
1920	Invention by Osman Yusuf Kenadid of the first script for the oral Somali language.
1934	'Walwal incident'—confrontation between Italian and Ethiopian forces at Walwal in the Ogaden which sparked off the Italo-Ethiopian war and led eventually to World War II.
1941	Allies defeat Italians and establish British Military Administration throughout Somali region, with the exception of French Somaliland.
1943	Somali Youth League, first major Somali nationalist party founded with the aid of the British Military Administration.
1946	British Foreign Secretary, Ernest Bevin, proposed that Somalilands should remain united as a single state and prepared for self-government.
1950	After rejection of the Bevin Plan, Somalia placed under UN Trusteeship, administered by Italy, with a ten year mandate. British Somaliland reverted to its former protectorate status, and the Ogaden was returned to Ethiopian control.
26 June 1960	British Somaliland became independent
1st July 1960	Italian Somalia became independent and joined Somaliland to form the Somali Republic (Somalia).

1963	Ogaden insurrection followed by brief outbreak of fighting between Somalia and Ethiopia.
1963-1967	Somali guerrila campaign attempting to secure Somali independence from Kenya in the northeastern region.
21 Oct. 1969	Military coup led by army commander General Mohamed Siyad Barre, overthrew the civilian government of Mohamed Haji Ibrahim Egal. State becomes the 'Somali Democratic Republic' (SDR), and embraces 'scientific socialism'—with the assistance of the USSR.
1973/1974	National literacy campaigns using Latin script for writing Somali.
1974	Catastrophic drought and famine leads to large displacement of northern Somali nomads to agricultural and fishing 'collectives' in southern Somalia.
1977	Djibouti (French Somaliland, and then later designated by the French as French Coast of Afars & Issas) became independent under President Hassan Guleid, ethnic Somali. Ogaden nationalists rebelled against an Ethiopia weakened by revolution following Haile Selassie's overthrow.
1977/78	Somali-Ethiopian war. Soviet Union changed sides to aid Ethiopia, and was replaced in Somalia by the USA.
1978	Somali defeat, followed by influx of hundreds of thousands of Somali refugees. Abortive *coup* against Siyad.
1982	Formation of Somali Salvation Democratic Front (Mijerteyn) guerrilla forces in northeast, and Somali National Movement (Isaq) in northwest. Both based in Ethiopia.
1988	Peace accord between Ethiopia and Somalia led to intensification of SNM struggle in northwest.
1990	Siyad's divide and rule policies, arming his allies with his Western-supplied equipment to suppress his enemies led to general militarisation and disintegration of the Somali state.
January 1991	Siyad overthrown by United Somali Congress (Hawiye) guerrillas and chased out of Mogadishu by

	General Aideed. General 'clan-cleansing' of Mogadishu by USC forces, killing or driving out members of Darod clans associated with Siyad. Followed by power struggle between USC leaders and Ali Mahdi.
May 1991	SNM declares the 'Somaliland Republic' independent of Somalia and distances itself from southern conflict and devastation.
March 1992	Mogadishu ceasefire followed by gradual return of humanitarian agencies to relieve spreading famine in southern Somali war zone.
April 1992	First UN special envoy appointed with prospect of UN security force to protect aid workers.
October 1992	UN launched '100 day action programme' and UN special envoy was forced to resign because of his justified criticism of UN operations.
December 1992	UN Resolution 794 authorised use of all necessary means to secure humanitarian relief, and US-led operation Restore Hope, involving 30,000 US and other troops, began its peace-keeping role in Somalia.
Jan & Mar 1993	Peace conferences in Addis Ababa. Leaders of militia groups signed agreements binding themselves to disarm and maintain peace, subject to heavy sanctions.
May 1993	Operation Restore Hope hands over to UNOSOM II under Security Council resolution 814, which provided for a multi-national force of 28,000 military personnel and 3,000 civilians.
5 June 1993	Aideed's forces ambushed Pakistani UN contingent, killing over 20 Blue Helmets. Admiral Howe, UN special envoy in charge of UNOSOM II, declared Aideed a wanted outlaw and launched attacks on Aideed strongholds in Mogadishu. Aideed's forces retaliated with a guerrilla campaign against UN troops.
1993	While these conferences for southern Somali leaders and warlords were proceeding, reaching conclusions that would never be implemented, the crucial state-forming Borama conference was held at that town in Somaliland.
(October)	Aideed's forces shot down several Black Hawk helicopters and humiliated survivors, causing huge furore at US casualties (subject of an American book and

film). New US President Clinton was forced to announce total US withdrawal by 31 March 1994.

1995   The UN exodus proceeded relatively smoothly and was immediately followed in Mogadishu by extensive looting, as a new generation of warlords seized abandoned resources and prepared to assert strategic dominance.

1996   Aideed was killed in battle over control of banana exports between his Habar Gidir clan and Abgal; southern Somalia reverted to 'normal' pattern of conflict and insecurity.

1997   Following over a year's conflict over control of airport revenue in Hargeisa, Somaliland re-established peace and order and Mohamed Haji Ibrahim Egal was elected for a further five-year term as Somaliland President.

1998   A Mijerteyn conference at Garoe established the 'new Puntland state of Somalia', which unlike Somaliland has not claimed complete independence from Somalia.

2000   The new Somali President of Djibouti, with UN support, launched a new Somalia peace conference at Arta with, for the first time, 'representatives' officially on a clan basis. In the absence of machinery to check whether or not the resulting 'delegates' were actually accredited clan representatives, this issue bedevilled the whole process. In fact 60 per cent were former members of Muhammad Siyad Barre's Assembly, which had been personally selected by the dictator. These people appointed one of their number, an ex-minister under Siyad, Abdulqasim Salad Hassan, a Habar Gidir politician who campaigned for Hawiye unity, as 'Transitional National President', hoping he could hold things together and establish his political authority in southern Somalia at least. In fact, following the usual segmentary trajectory, Abdulqasim and his militias never managed to control (fitfully) more than a couple of streets in Mogadishu.

2002   A new international Somalia 'peace conference' was organised by the EC and UN, as usual outside So-

127

malia, this time at Mbagathi (Kenya), and with the usual top-down assumptions and battery of supporting 'experts' whose especial distinction was failing to grasp the fundamentally decentralised character of Somali politics. Since the previous international effort (Arta) which had collapsed was supposedly based on traditional clan leaders, the formula here was to pass the baton to the warlords. So, as wide a group of warlords as possible (some of them accused by members of the Somali public of being war criminals) was desperately scraped together by EU diplomats in Kenya. With massive bribery and corruption, and more than a year's riotous debate, those attending the meeting, again comprising clan quotas, managed to 'elect' a 'transitional federal government' under the Ethiopian candidate, Abdillahi Yusuf, a renowned guerrilla leader and warlord, formerly President of Puntland.

2005   The transitional federal government moved back to Somalia.

2006   In Mogadishu a home-grown local association of Islamic clerics, based on mushrooming Islamic courts, gradually ousted criminal warlords (some supported by the US to 'fight Islamic terrorism') and re-established law and order for the first time since 1990. It wrested Mogadishu's airport and main seaport from the control of warlords, repaired those public utilities and opened them to general use. By June life in Mogadishu had miraculously returned to pre-war normality. Overplaying their hand, these Islamic groups threatened the Ethiopian-installed TFG president, calling him an infidel, and Ethiopians (with US complicity) increased their military support for the TFG.

2007   The TFG finally moved into Mogadishu with overwhelming Ethiopian (and US) military support, rekindling insurrection in southern Somalia. Hundreds of thousands of civilians fled Mogadishu.

APPENDIX 4

REFUGEES AND DIASPORA

- Refugees: estimated global number: 2.0 million approx.
- Main countries of asylum have been first, those which neighboured Somalia—Kenya, Ethiopia and to a lesser extent Djibouti; Arab countries, especially Yemen, which some minority groups considered the site of their ancestral homes and where they had had long trading and family links.
- Conditions in these refugee camps have been described as particularly harsh, refugees being subjected to inhuman treatment. Rape occurred regularly, and officials who were running the camps were often unscrupulous in their demands for sexual favours.
- Tendency in dispersal to coalesce in new locations around clan and ethnic groupings.
- Main countries of Somali communities abroad: North America: Canada and US Europe: UK, Holland, Finland, Scandinavian countries; Middle East: Egypt, Gulf States; and Saudi Arabia; Australia and New Zealand.

In the late 1980s Somalis, mainly Isaqis from Somaliland, began to flee over the border into Ethiopia to escape the bombing and destruction of their towns and villages by the Siyad Barre Regime—a bombing and straffing campaign that was intended to bring to heel the northern clans who were in rebellion against the increasingly tyrannical rule of the regime.[1] UNHCR refugee camps were opened in eastern Ethiopia, the largest being near the village of Hartisheikh. Some refugees with the means to do so travelled on to seek sylum further afield and to join

---

1   'Somalia: A government at war with its own people' *Africa Watch*, 1990.

relatives living outside the country. Some went to the Gulf States where there were communities of Somali migrant labourers, whilst many others sought the help of relatives in the UK, where there were long-established communities of Somalis in some of Britain's major seaports—a legacy of British colonial links with Somalis from the former British Somaliland Protectorate and the Aden Colony.[2]

Opposition to the regime was widespread, and by January 1991 the Barre government in Mogadishu had fallen, and Somalia was in the grip of civil war. The already desperate situation of ordinary people was further exacerbated when famine subsequently swept the country, and by 1992 close to one million Somalis had fled to neighbouring countries.[3] The primary routes into exile were overland to Kenya and Ethiopia, and to a lesser extent Djibouti, or by small boats down the coast to Kenya. A favoured route for the Benadiri Somalis, with strong traditions of origin in southern Arabia, was via Bossaso on the northern coast of Somalia and then to Bir Ali in Yemen, 300 km across the Gulf of Aden.[4] In the years since 1991, these countries have continued to be first place of sanctuary for Somali refugees, most of whom hoped to travel on to another country.

While the stream of Somalis fleeing persecution and mayhem in the south of the country continued unabated throughout the 1990s and beyond, in the north, the breakaway Somaliland Republic (which had

---

2 Aden, a coaling station on the shipping route between Indian and Britain had always been well populated by Somalis from the British Somaliland Protectorate, working as labourers for the British fleet, constituting the core pool of domestic staff for the British colonists, not to mention second and third generation Christian-educated Somali families who worked as clerks and judges in the Colony.

3 By the beginning of October 1992, Kenya alone hosted approximately 412,000 registered refugees and it was estimated that another 100,000 unregistered refugees were living in the country. More than 300,000 of these were Somalis (Gallagher & Forbes Martin 1992: 16).

4 Even though the Bossaso-Yemen route has proved to be a treacherous route, with many perishing on the crossing, Bossaso continues to be a point of departure, and today not just for Somalis but now for Eritreans and Ethiopians. Travel is in small open fishing boats unfit for purpose and overcrowded and even tied up to reduce movement in the overcrowded boats. Regularly passengers are thrown overboard at gunpoint, a mile or so off the Yemen coast by the traffickers who wish to avoid being caught by Yemen authorities. Many refugees, unable to swim, did not survive in the shark-infested waters.

pulled out of the union in the first months of the civil war (May 1991)), was putting in place new state structures, and working on reconciliation of its clan groupings. The political stability that was thus achieved in the course of the decade saw the gradual return of Somaliland families from exile, and was symbolised by the official closure in 2004 of Hart-isheikh—once the largest refugee camp in the world. With the collapse of Mogadishu under the Ethiopian onslaught in support of President Abdillahi Yusuf in 2007/8, as hundreds of thousands of southern Somalis fled, for the first time, many thousands found refuge in Somaliland, a state whose security and public services astounded them.

In southern Somalia, the periodic voluntary repatriation programmes by the UNHCR during periods of relative calm notwithstanding, and despite regular forced repatriation of Somalis by neighbouring country governments (in particular by Yemen and Kenya), these did nothing to reduce the overall Somali refugee numbers, but merely contributed to a revolving door effect as each new upsurge of violent factional fighting in Somalia sent new waves of people fleeing for their lives. With the intractable conflicts at home, the numbers of Somali refugees in the world continued to rise throughout the late 1990s and 2000s.[5]

Special case of refugees from minority communities

Somalis who have suffered disproportionately in the conflict are those belonging to a variety of ethnic or clan groups that were neither part of, nor allied to the numerically and politically dominant clans.[6] Most of these people have their roots in southern Somalia rather than the country as a whole, and include the urbanite Rer Hamar and Rer Brava from the Benadir coastal towns, the Bantu-Jareer cultivators living in the vicinity of either the Shebelle or Juba rivers, the Bajuni fisher people from Kismayu and the offshore islands, and the many and varied occupational caste groups spread throughout the Somali-inhabited territories. These low status people go by different names in different parts of the coun-

---

5   In March 2007 UNHCR issued figures of 350,000 Somali Refugees in neighbouring countries, and an estimated 400,000 internally displaced persons (IDPs). UN refugee statistics do not include unregistered refugees who are living clandestinely outside of the camps as illegal immigrants, nor those who have become absorbed into local life. But new refugees continue to arrive,

6   Refer to Cassanelli 'Victims and Vulnerable Groups'

131

try, names that are often synonymous with occupation. There has been longstanding prejudice against such groups by those of the dominant culture, who regard them as being different and 'not proper Somalis'. In the lawless chaos that characterised Somalia following the unravelling of state structures, old prejudices received their full expression. And human rights abuses were perpetrated with impunity.[7] In the case of the Benadiris, for example, as a trading community they were believed to be wealthy; and being an unarmed and unwarlike group they became easy targets for militias loyal to the different warlords, and armed bandits loyal to nobody : homes and businesses were destroyed, women and girls were raped in front of male relatives, and countless were slaughtered. Whilst the majority of those who could do so sought asylum elsewhere, a residual core of the community sought to remain in their home areas, not just because they lacked the means to escape, but in some instances as a deliberate expression of peaceful resistance to the attempts by majority clan groups at ethnic cleansing.

The Diaspora

The Somali civil war thus led to the modern day dispersal of the Somali nation. The Somalis are the largest African community in the United Arab Emirates, where Somali businesses line the streets of the Dubai city centre, Deira—a testimony to the Somalis' entrepreneurial spirit. As well as in Africa and the Middle East, there are also thriving communities of ethnic Somalis in all the main cities of Western Europe and North America. Here also they find employment in small businesses, telephone shops, internet suppliers, IT work, and with taxi firms. Other men find work as bus drivers.

In the United Kingdom, the 2001 census reported almost 44,000 Somalis, but later estimates range between 95,000 and 250,000 Harris, 2004). London, Cardiff, Liverpool, Manchester, Sheffield, Birmingham, Leeds, and Leicester are home to the largest concentrations of Somalis. The first three have the oldest Somali ethnic communities in Britain.

In the rest of Europe, there are significant Somali communities in the Netherlands, Norway, Denmark, and Sweden. An interesting case of Somali European immigration is in Finland which, although it is one of the most ethnically homogeneous European countries, and where im-

---

7   These have been well documented by UN specialist agencies, NGOs, and
    human rights organisations such as Amnesty and Human Rights Watch.

migrants consitute only a small part of Finnish society, yet Somali refugees here are by far the largest group of people of non-European origin. The basis of the Finland Somali phenomenon comprised the university students in the-then-Soviet universitites, who became stranded with the collapse of the Somali state. They started arriving in Finland in 1991 as political refugees. Later, more refugees arrived directly from Somalia in a programme of family unification. Their effect on the Finnish landscape is demonstrated in it being among the first European countries where ethnic Somalis (who, it must be said, come from a highly politicised culture) have made their way in local politics, and have been elected to council seats in several cities, including Helsinki and Turku.

In North America, Toronto and Minneapolis have the largest Somali populations, followed by Columbus, Washington DC, Ottawa, and Atlanta, although they are scattered throughout the continent in small numbers. Many refugees have been granted citizenship in their country of asylum in view of their length of residence, or as a result of managed resettlement programmes, and have become part of national statistical tables that are disaggregated in other ways than by immigration. Among refugees who have been considered for permanent resettlement by ethnicity the case of the Bantu-Jareer Somalis is unique. Somali Bantu-Jareer form a marginalized and persecuted minority who are descended largely from a former slave population that lived in Somalia for over two centuries, but had never been fully accepted as 'true Somali' by the dominant clans. With a distinctly separate ethnicity, lifestyle, and appearance, the Bantu-Jareer had endured continual marginalization, despite for the most part having taken on board mainstream Somali culture. A few, however, had retained strong African identity and language, and traced their origins back to ancestors in east African tribes further south (in Tanzania and Mozambique); this was especially so of the Bantu from the once-forested Juba river valley, referrred to as *Wagosha* "peope of the forest", or more pejoratively as *adon* and *habash*, which translate as "slave".

In the mid 1990s Bantu Somalis from refugee camps in northern Kenya were offered resettlement opportunities in Tanzania—which many considered to be their ancestral homeland. Around three thousand took up the offer, and the Tanzanian government allocated them land for their resettlement at Chogo and offered them citizenship.

In 1999, the United States designated exiled Somali Bantus as a persecuted class of people who were deserving of resettlement in America, and approved the resettlement of approximately 12,000 Bantu refugees

133

from camps in Kenya. Though the programme was delayed somewhat by the events of Nine-Eleven (2001) and the extremely rigorous screening measures that were put in place, because of concerns that Islamist terrorists might try to use the visa programme to gain entry to the United States, the first Somali Bantu refugees arrived in Denver, Colorado from Kakuma camp in Kenya in 2003. (It was reported that when the United States announced its decision to take in the Bantus, hundreds of other exiled Somalis suddenly declared themselves part of the underclass. Somali refugees as far away as Nairobi boarded buses for the Kakuma transit camp to try to buy their way into Bantu families.)

In Europe, where there is free movement across borders for EU nationals, many who have acquired national status in one country prefer then to transfer their residence to another EU country, most markedly to the UK, where the English language is a strong attraction, as well as the presence of significant communities from all clans. The nomadic instinct that is so distinctive of Somali mainstream culture remains strong even in diaspora, as is the predilection to coalesce around clan, in consequence of which the degree of mobility is high.

Hawala

Overall attachment to the mother country remains strong, as is most obviously demonstrated in the flourishing *hawala* or Alternative Remittance system (*hawala* in Arabic means 'trust'), whereby money can be made available internationally without actually moving it. In the absence of governance and a banking sector in Somalia, *hawala* remittance firms are the only available channels for Somalis to send money to family members and relatives. The *hawala* market is indispensable to families responsible to and dependent on family ties, and in 2006 the flow of money was estimated to be between US$750 million and US $1 billion annually.

INDEX

Abdille Hassan, Muhammad 5, 16-20, 21, 29-30
Abgal 73, 80
Abo Liberation Front 64
Abshir, Muhammad 32, 38, 100, 101-2
Adde, Mahamud Muse 103-6
Addis Ababa 29, 44
Aden 28, 130
Afars 43, 56
Afgoi 10, 19, 74
Af-Maymay 3, 6, 62
Agricultural Development Corporation 40
agriculture 25-6, 40-1, 48, 51, 58-64, 66
Ahmadiya 16, 19
Aideed, General Muhammad Farah 73, 74, 78-80, 101
Aideed, Hussein 80-1
Alliance for the Restoration of Peace and Counter-Terrorism 85-91
al-Qaida 86, 105
Arab countries 41, 56, 57, 64, 82, 129
Arab League 42
Arabs 8-9, 20
Arta conference 81-2

Arteh, Omar 74
Asmara 43
asylum seekers in West 8, 71, 104, Appendix 4
Atto, Osman Ali 80
Awash river 1
Aways, Sheikh Hassan Daahir 86

Baidoa 6, 74, 84, 88, 107
Bajuni 131
Bakol 107
Bale 43, 65
bananas 30, 40, 59
Bantu 4, 6, 11, 131, 133-4
Bantu-Jareer 6, 7, 131, 133
Bardera 19
Bargal 105
Barre, see Siyad Barre
Bay 59-60, 107
Benadir 5, 8-11, 131-2
Benadiri 8, 15, 130, 131-2
Berbera 95, 96, 99
Biamal 5
Bioley 17
'Black Hawk down' incident 79
Boni 6
Borama 5, 93-5, 96
Borana 1
Bossaso 100, 103, 106, 130

135

Brava 2, 11, 63, 86
Britain 8, 17-19, 28-33, 34, 36, 85, 98, 130, 132; British Military Administration 31-3
British Somaliland 17, 29-34, 37, 130
Bunda, Nasib 6
Bur Heibe 6
Burao 96, 97
Burton, Sir Richard 22-3, 29

Campaign for Rural Development 41-2
Central Rangelands Development Project 53
Christian churches 30-1
CIA 85
'civil society' 81
clan and family systems 3-5, 11-16, 27-8, 35-6, 40, 49-56, 75-7, 90-1, Appendix 1
Clinton, President Bill 79
conflicts in southern Somalia 1988-2008 71-91, 99, 129-31, (chronology) 125-8
constitutions 35, 45, 97
Corfield, Richard 18-19
corruption 72, 83, 98
coup attempt of April 1978 45, 51, 67
Cuba 43, 44

Darod 4, 5, 6, 40, 46, 49, 67, 68, 72, 73, 74, 82, 84, 90, 94, 99-100, 101, 106, 107
'Dervish War' 16-20, 21, 29-30
Diaspora 132-4
Digil 5, 11, 12, 14, 51, 59, 61-2, 63, 69
Digil Mirifle 4, 7, 25, 82, 84, 107

Dir 4-5, 33, 82, 97
Dire Dawa 29
Djibouti 1, 29, 32, 36, 42-3, 44, 71, 95, 129, 130; peace conferences 74, 81-2
drought of 1974-75 41-2, 52, 53, 62-4, 66
Dubai 132
'Dugleh' 40, 46
Dulbahante 40, 46, 49, 69, 74, 77, 94, 99, 101, 106

Edna Adan hospital 99
education 31, 41, 98-9
Egal, Mohamed Haji Ibrahim 34, 37
Eritrea 28, 43, 88, 95, 106
Esa 5, 72
Ethiopia 1, 2, 17-19, 21, 24, 28-33, 36-7, 42-5, 56, 64-9, 71-2, 74, 81, 83, 84, 86, 88-90, 95, 96, 97, 99, 100, 103, 107, 129, 130, 131; Italian occupation 31-2; intervention in Somalia (2007) 88-90, 131
EU 81, 83-5, 107, 134
Eyle 6

family life 11-16, 49-56
famine 78, 130
Finland 132-3
fishing 63, 64, 66, 104-5, 131-2
France 28-9, 42

Gadabursi 5, 72, 77, 97
Galbed 63
Galje'el 62
Galkayu 103
Garowe 102-3, 106
Garre 62

Gedo 73
Geedi, Ali 84
Geledi 19
Germany, East 44, 45
Gulf States 57, 64, 132
Gurey, Ahmed 2

Habar Gidir 73, 74, 80, 82, 90-1,
    101
Habar Ja'lo 94, 96
Habar Yunis 94, 96
Haile Selassie 33, 42
Hamarweyn 9-10
Harar 2, 3, 5, 28-9, 44, 58
Hargeisa 16, 96, 97, 98
Harti 99, 101
Hartisheikh camp 129, 131
Hassan, Abdiqasim Salad 82, 86
Haud 33, 58
hawala 134
Hawiye 4-5, 33, 59, 62, 72, 73, 77,
    82, 84, 86, 90, 107
health care 22, 99
Hersi, Mohamed Siyad (Morgan)
    78

IGAD 81, 83
Isa 77
Isaq 4-5, 52, 68, 71-2, 74-5, 77,
    96, 97
Ise, Abdillahi 34
Islam 1-3, 11, 16-23, 85-90, 98
Islamic Courts Union 21, 85-90
Italy 10, 28-34, 38, 82, 90; colonial
    administration 30-3, 34, 36
Ittihad, al- 86, 100, 103

Jama, Jama Ali 103
Jareer=Bantu-Jareer, *q.v.*
Jigjiga 30, 58

Jowhar 80, 84
Juba river 3, 5, 6, 19, 51, 63, 131,
    133

Kahin, Dahir Riyale 97
Kenya 1, 5, 24, 29, 36, 37, 74, 83,
    88, 89, 129, 130, 131, 133,
    134
Kismayu 8, 11, 74, 86, 89, 101
Kulmiye, General Husseyn 48

literacy campaigns 23, 41
livestock rearing, *see* pastoralism
livestock trade, *see under* trade
low-status groups 6-11, 131-2

Mahdi, Ali 73-5, 80
malaria 22
Marrehan 46, 49, 50, 69, 76
marriage 14-16
Masleh, General 69
Massawa 43
Mbagathi talks and Transitional
    Federal Government 83-5,
    88-91, 106-7
medicine (traditional) 22
Menelik 29
Mengistu Haile Mariam, Colonel
    43, 71, 100
Merca 3, 8, 11, 86
Midgans 7
migrant labour 57-8, 64, 130
Mijerteyn 49, 51, 67, 72, 77, 84,
    100-2, 105
missions (Christian) 30-1
Mogadishu 2, 5, 10, 29, 32, 33,
    38, 44, 72, 73, 74-5, 77, 80,
    82, 84, 86, 88-90, 102, 131
Morgan (Mohamed Siyad Hersi)
    78

National Security Courts 45
National Security Service 40, 45, 46, 48, 74
nomads, *see* pastoralism

Oakley, Robert 82
Ogaden 5, 17, 31, 33, 36-7, 42-5, 46, 52, 58, 66, 68, 71-4, 98
Ogaden National Liberation Front 71
Ogaden war 1977-78 42-5, 64, 68
Organisation of African Unity 42
Orientation Centres 40
Oromo 1, 4, 16-17, 29, 43, 58, 64-5
Oromo Liberation Front 64
Osman Mahamud 100
Osman, Adan Abdulle 33

Pakistan 79
pastoralism 3, 7, 12-14, 25-6, 41-2, 50, 51-6, 58, 62-5
peace talks 74, 81, 93-5, 97, 99
piracy 105
poetry 7, 18-19, 23
polygyny 11-13
Puntland 5, 83, 89, 100-8

Qadiriya 16, 17, 20
qat 24, 87
Qoniin, Sharif Yusuf Al- (Qonton Barkhadle) 16-17

Rahanweyn 4, 5, 12, 14, 51, 59, 61-2, 63
Rahanweyn Resistance Army 107
refugees 1, 47, 64-7, 71-2, 74, 99, 104, Appendix 4

relief 41, 66-7, 78
remittances 57-8, 99, 134
Rer Benadir 8-9
Rer Hamar 5, 9-11, 131
Revolutionary Councils 48
Revolutionary Youth Centres 39
Russia/Soviet Union 28-9, 32, 34, 37, 39, 42-5, 47, 133

Saad 91
Sab 4, 7
Salihiya 16-17
Samatar, General Muhammad Ali 7-8, 69
Samatar, Professor Said 86
Sanag 2, 94
Saudi Arabia 86, 87, 95, 98
Shangani 9-10
'Sharti Gudud' 107
Shebelle river 3, 5, 6, 10, 51, 59, 63, 84, 131
Shermarke, Dr Abdirashi Ali 33-4, 37
Shidle 6
Sidamo 65
Siyad Barre, President Muhammad 7, 8, 10, 13, 15, 32, 38-49, 67-9, 71-4, 75-6, 82, 90, 100, 129-30
slaves 4, 6, 11, 30, 60
social institutions and traditions 24-6, 49-55, *see also* clan and family systems
socialism 13, 39-42
Somali language 3-4, 17, 24; adoption of Roman script 41
Somali National Movement (SNM) 68-9, 71-6, 93-5
Somali Patriotic Movement (SPM) 73

Somali Refugee Commission 66
Somali Revolutionary Socialist Party (SRSP) 45-7
Somali Salvation Democratic Front (SSDF) 67-9, 71, 77, 84, 100-1
Somali Youth League (SYL) 32, 35, 37
Somaliland Republic 5, 14, 15, 52, 74-5, 82, 91, 93-100, 106, 131
Sool 106
South Africa 97
Soviet Union/Russia 28-9, 32, 34, 37, 39, 42-5, 47, 133
Sudan 28, 30
Swahili 3, 6, 60

Tanzania 133
Togdheer 53
trade in livestock and livestock products 41, 56-7, 95, 105
Transitional Federal Government (TFG) 83-5, 88-91, 106-7
Transitional National Government 82
Tumals 7-8
Tunni 11

UNHCR 67, 129, 131
UNITAF 78-9
United Nations 32, 34, 78-83, 90, 93, 95, 96

United Somali Congress (USC) 73-7
UNOSOM 78, 82
UNOSOM II   78-80, 93, 96
United Arab Emirates 132
USA 7, 37, 43-4, 78-82, 83, 85-6, 88-90, 98, 103, 104, 133-4
Uways, Sheikh 17

Wa'adan 11
Wahhabis 20, 87
Wako Goto 43
Warsangeli 77, 94, 101
Walwal incident 31
water supply (rural) 53, 55
Western Somali Liberation Front 43-4, 64-5, 68
women's position and roles 11-16, 21
World Bank 53
World War, Second 31-2

Yalahow, Muuse Soodi 80, 84
Yemen 44, 104-5, 129, 130
Yibir 7
Yusuf Muhamad 19
Yusuf, Col. Abdillahi 83-4, 87, 88-90, 100, 101-7, 131

Zeila 2, 3, 5
Zenawi, Meles 84